the
Townsend
eight

Published by

**Ferry Publications, PO Box 33,
Ramsey, Isle of Man IM99 4LP**

Tel: +44 (0) 1624 898445 Fax: +44 (0) 1624 898449

Email: ferrypubs@aol.com   Website: www.ferrypubs.co.uk

Miles Cowsill · John Hendy

Acknowledgements

Photographs and extra information used in this publication have been provided by FotoFlite of Ashford, Andrew Jones, John May, Anthony Meads, Mike Louagie, Frank Lose, Frank Heine, Ulrich Streich, Dieter Streich, Marko Stampehl and Wim Stout (Technical Director of van der Giessen-de Noord NV). Gary Andrews from Larne has kindly supplied details concerning the ships' North Channel service while Henk van der Lugt has followed Dutch sources relating to their building.

The *Free Enterprise's* former Assistant Purser Rozelle Raynes has kindly granted permission to use material from her book 'A Boat called *Martha*' (published by Shaun Tyas, Donington in 2001).

The input of a number of former Townsend Masters has added a professional dimension to this manuscript and their willingness to participate is greatly appreciated. Captain Vic Ridges served on all eight FE ships and typically reacted with enthusiasm and gusto to the suggestion that he might like to offer his memories which as usual are as pertinent as they are amusing. Captain Jim (Jas. W.) Martin served in all but the FE VIII and also found time within his busy schedules to answer questions and remember the 'Townsend Eight.' Captain Alan Ewart-James joined Townsend Thoresen following the take-over of P&O Normandy Ferries in January 1985 and his personal memories are also grateful y acknowledged. Captain Bob Blowers was latterly Senior Master of the *Pride of Calais/ P&OSL Calais* but gained his short-sea experience in five of the 'Townsend Eight.' His detailed reminiscences of the early days add great

Above: The *Free Enterprise VI* heads out of Dover Eastern Docks for Zeebrugge in October 1984. *(John Hendy)*

Below: P&O's *Pride of Canterbury* is seen entering Boulogne during her last season on the route from Dover. *(John Hendy)*

colour to the story and as with his former collagues, his input is warmly received and appreciated.

Finally a tremendous word of thanks to Commodore John E. Dawson (known to all as 'Jack') who served the company from 1948 until his retirement in 1976. He introduced all but the FE II into service and also stood by the *Viking Viscount* at Alborg. In recognition of his outstanding service and major contribution to the company's fortunes, in 1972 he was made Fleet Commodore. Even at the remarkable age of 89, he happily agreed to provide the Foreword to this book and eagerly looked towards its publication date. It was also Commodore Dawson who contacted the ships' designer James Ayres who was also only too pleased to assist in clearing up a number of technical matters. Our grateful thanks to all who have so generously contributed towards this volume.

Miles Cowsill
Ramsey,
Isle of Man.

John Hendy
Ivychurch,
Kent.

PUBLISHERS'S NOTE

The diary entries for the eight 'Free Enterprise' class vessels serve to show the main events of their careers but are by no means claimed to be definitive. They are simply as good as John Hendy's available records and it is acknowledged that gaps do exist. What we have attempted to achieve is to capture the life and times of the eight ferries through the diary entries, our excellent photographic archive and through some rich and varied personal memories. Readers able to add to the story are encouraged to contact Ferry Publications and it would be good to think that their contributions might eventually be included in a future edition.

The *Free Enterprise VI* arrives at Dover's berth 3 from Zeebrugge as the *Free Enterprise II* passes through the eastern entrance from Calais. (*Miles Cowsill*)

Foreword

by Commodore J.E. Dawson

I am delighted to be asked to write a Foreword to the story of 'The Townsend Eight.' It all started with the m.v. *Free Enterprise* which later became the *Free Enterprise I*. I joined her when building in Holland. A new house flag depicting three ships had been designed which at that time (1962) was thought a little ambitious, if not arrogant, as we were competitors to B.R. Not so, however, as we finished up with eight! I became Master of each one of them (excepting the *Free Enterprise II*) from building to sailing. At that time they were the latest in technology, having bow thrusters and variable pitch propellers. They were a joy to handle and were very happy ships. The crews were also very efficient and happy and none ever wanted to leave.

I have many recollections of a variety of events too numerous to mention. To name but two I recall to memory: On a fine day one August, when the sea was a flat calm and as blue as a lake, a small cabin cruiser was sighted. There was no one on deck and as it appeared to be abandoned we altered course, slowing down as we came alongside. Many of the passengers had come up on deck and we all gazed down at the boat to find ourselves looking at a young couple sunbathing in the nude. We later discovered that they were on their honeymoon and had not heard or seen us arrive. Everyone on deck cheered and with a couple of blasts on our siren we sped away leaving them looking somewhat flustered!

On a sadder occasion, I was conducting a short burial after stopping the ship in mid-Channel. There was a full gale blowing at the time and as I consigned the casket containing my friend's ashes to the sea, I lost both my cap *and* my false teeth. This slightly relieved the solemnity of the occasion and everyone present was amused at my expense!

Some of my shipmates will have

Commodore Dawson on the bridge wing of the *Free Enterprise VIII*.

other memories to tell. All this happened over 25 years ago when I retired as Commodore. With age memories fade, so enjoy the book as much as I have. It brought back many memories.

The *Free Enterprise V* outward bound from Dover. *(FotoFlite)*

Introduction

Townsend's eight 'Free Enterprise' ships were originally built for their owners' services from Dover to Calais and, after 1966, Zeebrugge. As an expansionist Townsend (then owned by George Nott Industries) embraced Thoresen in 1968 and the European Ferries Group was formed, so the 'Free Enterprises' were also seen at Southampton and later Portsmouth. The acquisition of the Atlantic Steam Navigation Co. in 1971 also saw units running on the North Channel link between Cairnryan and Larne whilst refits and charters brought appearances at Felixstowe, Newhaven and the Channel Islands.

Between 1974 and 1980 the shores of the British Isles were graced by the presence of all eight 'Free Enterprise' class ships. The diminutive *Free Enterprise* of 1962 saw 18 years of service in British waters and following her sale has worked in the eastern Mediterranean for an even longer period. And longevity has been a feature of every member of the class, each of which remained in existence (if not in operation) as this book was being written.

Captain Dawson with George Nott, Townsend's Managing Director.

Above: On board the *Free Enterprise I* looking aft towards the inner harbour at Calais. The *Compiegne* and the *Cote d'Azur* are at the Gare Maritime. *(John Hendy's collection)*
Below: The *Free Enterprise II* berthing at Dover's Prince of Wales' Pier following her maiden voyage on 22nd May 1965. *(John Hendy)*

The Townsend fleet of 1966 with the *Free Enterprise II* (left), *Free Enterprise I* (centre) and *Free Enterprise III* in the Camber at Dover. *(Commodore J.E. Dawson's collection)*

As with the pioneer vessel, the second and third ships were also 'one-offs' before the growth in freight saw the introduction of a standard design with the *Free Enterprise IV* in 1969. Thereafter in the further vessels this was modified in terms of engine output and vehicle deck layout and with the *Free Enterprise VIII* in service in 1974, the series was complete.

Further traffic growth and advances required a new and completely radical rethink and this was eventually forthcoming with the *Spirit of Free Enterprise* trio of 1980. The entry into service of these ships saw the withdrawal of the first three of the 'Townsend Eight' which collectively served the briefest careers of

7

the series. The acquisition of the P&O Normandy Ferries Dover - Boulogne service in 1985 unexpectedly extended the operational careers of the FE IV, FE V and FE VIII for periods of between eighteen months and seven years.

The other two ships of the series (FE VI and FE VII) were rebuilt and stretched to carry more freight on the Zeebrugge link but were withdrawn following the route's closure to passenger traffic and the entry into service of the new European class freighters. In 1992 they were switched to the North Channel for the remainder of their service.

With the withdrawal from service of the former *Free Enterprise VII* - by then the *Pride of Rathlin* - in September 2000, the 38 year connection was broken. But in the following summer the former

The *Free Enterprise III* in the Baudouin Canal at Zeebrugge in 1967. *(Andrew Jones)*

This view from the cliffs shows the *Free Enterprise I* clearing the eastern exit of Dover Harbour on 27th April 1969. *(Andrew Jones)*

Free Enterprise V reappeared on the Ostend - Ramsgate link as the Cypriot-registered *Laburnum* thereby insuring the restoration of the 'Free Enterprise' lineage.

The success of Townsend Car Ferries and of the 'Free Enterprise' ships was mirrored by the growth of road-borne freight which came to revolutionise the method by which heavy goods were shipped. Within the 38 years under review there was a complete reformation in the design and purpose of short-sea ships from small seasonal car ferries carrying tourist traffic to huge year-round operation, double-decked, freight carriers. It is certainly worth reflecting that in the year the *Free Enterprise* entered service in 1962, some 2,055 freight units passed through the Port of Dover.

the **Townsend** eight

A splendid view of the *Free Enterprise VI* at full speed en route to Dover from Zeebrugge. *(FotoFlite)*

The *Free Enterprise VII* is seen inward bound following her jumboisation for the Zeebrugge service. *(John May)*

In 1974, during which time the *Free Enterprise VIII* came on station, this had risen to 237,837 and by 1989 over one million pieces of freight annually crossed the Dover Strait through the port.

The 'Free Enterprises' were designed by Mr. James Ayres, Townsend's naval architect and his energy and vision was backed by the rest of the board led successively by George Nott, Roland Wickenden and, after his untimely death following the launch of the *Free Enterprise VII*, his brother Keith Wickenden. They saw an opportunity to lead the way and to capitalise in the trade which they had collectively anticipated and helped create.

In 1962 the *Free Enterprise* was but a thorn in the side of Townsend's competitors at Dover. By the time that the *Free Enterprise VIII* entered service twelve years later, Townsend Thoresen were the English Channel's number one operator and a considerable force to be reckoned with. Here indeed was a transport revolution!

As with all good ships, eventually the 'Townsend Eight' were victims of their own success and this publication seeks to celebrate their significant contribution to the British ferry industry.

The **Pride of Hythe** at Calais in spring 1992 while covering for the **Pride of Kent**. *(John May)*

P&O EUROPEAN FERRIES

The European Ferries Group (trading as Townsend Thoresen since 1969) was taken over by the P&O Group in December 1986. Following the *Herald of Free Enterprise* disaster off Zeebrugge in the following March, the remaining ferries were immediately given P&O pale blue funnels.

In an effort to distance itself from the previous regime, P&O totally reorganised the company in October 1987 and created P&O European Ferries. At this time all Dover ships with 'Free Enterprise' in their names (apart from the *Free Enterprise IV*) were renamed with 'Pride of' prefixes and repainted in a sober navy blue livery.

P&O European Ferries greatly modernised and uprated the interiors of the remaining four 'Free Enterprise' ferries along with

An unusual view of a well-loaded *Free Enterprise IV* coming astern out of the eastern exit at Dover. *(FotoFlite)*

that of their more modern units.

As from 26th March 1990, Club Class lounges were introduced in the Observation Lounges aft of the funnels. This was the creation of First Class travel where for a £7.50 supplement, passengers could enjoy an exclusive lounge with free papers, coffee and other benefits. The fleet modernisation continued during the following winter when Peninsular Lounges and POSH Bars were added. Ships were given the 'traditional' treatment with brass fittings, etched glass and posters portraying the 'golden age' of P&O travel.

Above: The *Pride of Hythe* arriving at Boulogne. *(Mike Louagie)*
Below: The *Pride of Canterbury* (ex *Free Enterprise VIII*) leaves the outer harbour at Boulogne for Dover. *(John Hendy)*

The *Pride of Rathin* leaves the port of Larne for Scotland. *(Miles Cowsill)*

TOWNSEND   **TOWNSEND THORESEN**

LIVERIES

During their 38 years of service, the 'Townsend Eight' appeared in a number of liveries:

1962 - 'Caronia' green hulls and red, black topped funnels.
1965 - 'Townsend' (in red) added to the superstructure.
1972 - 'Townsend Thoresen' in small white letters on hulls. TTF logo appeared on funnels in pale green.
1974 - Dark green hulls adopted with company name in large white letters.
1976 - Thoresen orange adopted for all ships' hulls. Funnels eventually became dark green with orange TTF logo.
1984 - New TT logo, in white, introduced on funnels.
1987 - Following the 'Herald' disaster, from spring onwards, pale blue funnels with P&O flag logo.
1987 - From October, change to P&O European Ferries navy blue hull and funnel.

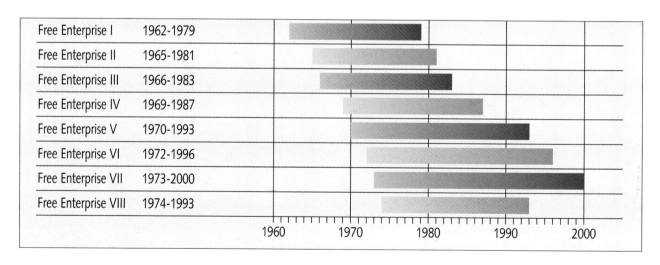

Free Enterprise I	1962-1979
Free Enterprise II	1965-1981
Free Enterprise III	1966-1983
Free Enterprise IV	1969-1987
Free Enterprise V	1970-1993
Free Enterprise VI	1972-1996
Free Enterprise VII	1973-2000
Free Enterprise VIII	1974-1993

The *Free Enterprise IV* at Dover's double-decked berth 4 loading for Calais. This 1972 picture shows the company trading name in small white letters. *(John Hendy)*

A classic end of pier view of the *Free Enterprise I* passing through the jetties at Calais for another crossing of the Dover Strait. *(Andrew Jones)*

Free Enterprise
Free Enterprise I

In 1961 all ferries which operated from British ports had black hulls and it was therefore assumed that the new *Free Enterprise* would also appear in this traditional livery. However, George Nott, the chairman of Coventry-based George Nott Industries and owner of Townsend Bros Car Ferries Ltd., was crossing the Dover Strait one day on the bridge of the *Halladale*. Away in the distance the Cunard cruise liner *Caronia* came into sight and Nott (who knew nothing whatsoever about ships) asked Captain Jack Dawson the name of the impressive-looking vessel. He expressed

A view from the cliffs at Dover that captures the **Free Enterprise** leaving Dover for Calais during her early career in the English Channel. *(Andrew Jones)*

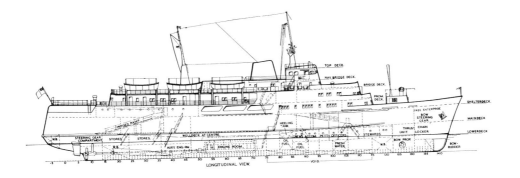

The new *Free Enterprise* arriving at Dover 's berth 2 for trials in April 1962. During her first season her name was painted white. *(Commodore J.E. Dawson's collection)*

Above: One of the side lounges aboard the **Free Enterprise**. *(Ferry Publications Library)*
Right: Duty Free shop on the **Free Enterprise**. *(Ferry Publications Library)*

a great liking for the Cunarder's pale green hull colouring and decided that his new ship should be similarly coated. Nott later even telephoned Cunard to ask from where they obtained their paint!

The non-stabilised *Free Enterprise* was not simply unique in her eye-catching bright livery. Her accommodation was unusually of the open-plan type and her vehicle deck headroom was as much as 14ft. which would enable high-sided lorries to be carried. Townsend had anticipated the growth of this traffic and were far-sighted in the ship's design although this extra dimension was slow to develop.

The £1 million *Free Enterprise* replaced the turbine steamer *Halladale* (ex HMS *Halladale*) which had completed her final voyage on 5th November 1961. The vessel had been built by A&J Inglis on the Clyde in 1944 as a River class frigate. Sold to Townsend in 1949 after conversion to car ferry use at Cork for £77,000, she had completed her maiden voyage on 7th April 1950 and had latterly provided accommodation for 388 passengers and 60 cars.

A careful eye from the bridge wing of **Free Enterprise I** as she arrives at Calais passing the SNCF vessel **Compiegne**. *(John Hendy's collection)*

1961

Keel laid on 7th August.

1962

Ship launched at IHC's N.V. Werf 'Gusto' Schiedam yard by Mrs. Bernice Nott (wife of the chairman of George Nott Industries) on 2nd February. Maiden voyage due on 12th April but under the command of Captain Jack Dawson this was delayed until 22nd April (just 8 months after the keel was laid).

In early August the ship had to return to Rotterdam with a damaged bow-rudder. During this time Townsend chartered the SNCF train ferry *Saint-Germain*. The *Free Enterprise* was again out of service on 7th August following damage when leaving Dover

for Calais. With the SNCF car ferry *Compiegne* also damaging a screw that day, there were no car ferries operating to Calais.

1963

The season commenced as early as 1st February. During the ship's first full year in service, 83,545 cars and 250,000 passengers were carried against the 27,487 cars and 86,744 passengers carried by the *Halladale* in her last season.

1964

On 26th July the ship collided with the East Pier at Calais resulting in a number of buckled plates. Exactly one month later

A view from the fo'c'sle of the **Free Enterprise I** arriving at Dover. At berth 2, the **Roi Baudouin** can be seen with the **Lord Warden** at the lay by berth. *(John Hendy's collection)*

This period view of the Camber shows (l. to r.) the British Railways' turbine steamers **Maid of Kent** and **Lord Warden** with the **Free Enterprise** prior to her entry into service. *(Commodore J.E. Dawson's collection)*

the ship was running on one screw and taking 4 hours per crossing. Returning from an overhaul at Amsterdam on 8th December, a broken bow rudder meant a return to the yard. SNCF's *Compiegne* was also on overhaul at this time and therefore all vehicle ferry sailings to Calais were suspended. With the *Free Enterprise II* under construction, the ship was given the suffix 'I'.

1965

On 20th January the ship snapped all mooring ropes at Dover in a fierce easterly gale.

1967

During April the ship was back in service after modifications at Schiedam. A duty-free bar was added, the bank was moved and

Looking forward from the *Free Enterprise II* on her press voyage to Calais with the *Free Enterprise I* at the port dressed overall on 19th May 1965. *(John Hendy)*

The *Free Enterprise I* arriving at berth 2 at the Eastern Docks in Dover. *(John Hendy)*

an new upper deck saloon for 60-80 passengers was constructed under the mainmast.

1968

Following an accident to the chartered Thoresen ferry *Viking II*, while deputising on the Zeebrugge link in mid-November, the *Free Enterprise I* was transferred to the Belgian service for three days. She was not a success.

1969

On 3rd February more bad weather saw the ship part lines at Calais during loading causing damage to the ramp as a result of which she missed a sailing.

1970

The AA's 'Drive' Magazine for summer 1970 said of the ship, "... A three course meal in the attractive dining room cost 15s 6d; the waiters were eager to please and there was a good range of hot and cold snacks available. Stairs from the boat deck are narrow and steep. Crew members were helpful and courteous and broadcast announcements were loud and clear in English and in French. The ship left three minutes late and arrived five minutes early. The last car was off twelve minutes after landfall".

1971

On 6th September the ship hit a dolphin and was holed when going astern to her berth at Calais. It took five hours to discharge her vehicles and eventually she sailed to Dover in ballast for repairs. Resumed service on 10th September. Ship called out of lay-up 11th-13th October to operate the Calais service vice the *Free Enterprise III* which was transferred to Zeebrugge vice the *Free Enterprise V*.

1972

Summer service to Calais with the *Free Enterprise III*. The ship ran aground at Calais on the evening on 13th November. After temporary repairs she left under tow for Vlissingen on 17th November.

1973

Summer Calais service with FE III and FE IV. With the *Free Enterprise III* off service with engine troubles on 17th December, the FE I was switched to the Zeebrugge route.

The *Free Enterprise I* laid-up at Calais in August 1976. *(John Hendy)*

1974

The ship went to lay-up on 21st October after which the *Free Enterprise III* (from Cairnryan) took her Calais schedules.

1975

Following the unsuccessful experiment with the *Free Enterprise III* in 1974, the ship was transferred to the Cairnryan - Larne service from 22nd May to operate with the *Bardic Ferry* and her sister the *Ionic Ferry*. Sailings were 14.00 and 21.30 from Cairnryan and 10.00 and 18.00 from Larne.

1976

The ship was spare and laid-up in Calais for the winter of 1975-76 and all the following summer when a 6 ship roster made her surplus to requirements. The ship was required to assist on two occasions: firstly during the summer vice the FE II which had gone off service with a damaged bow visor and secondly after the FE VI had collided with the pier at Calais during the autumn. Thereafter she spent the winter 1976-77 laid-up at Tilbury alongside the FE II.

1977

Left Tilbury in mid-February. With a 7 ship roster in 1977, the ship was reactivated to run the additional 11.35 and 17.35 sailings to Calais.

1978

Peak summer season saw the first three 'Free Enterprises' and the FE V on the Calais service in a similar pattern to 1977.

1979

The ship was at lay-up in Dover's Wellington Dock during the early part of the year. The summer period saw the first three 'Free Enterprises' in service together on the Calais route for the final time before the *Free Enterprise II* laid-up at Tilbury on 3rd September. She was back in service after refit for the pre-Christmas period on 1st November. With the *Spirit of Free Enterprise* nearing completion at Bremerhaven, Christmas Eve saw the ship's final sailings between Dover and Calais after which she was laid-up for the festive season in the Granville Dock, Dover (with the *Free Enterprise III* and P&O's *Lion*) before sailing to Tilbury to await sale.

An early view in Greek waters of the former FE I now renamed *Kimolos*. She is seen at Piraeus in 1981 after a late summer's journey through the Cyclades Islands. *(John May)*

1980

Ship sold to Greek operator Ventouris Sea Lines and sailed at 17.30 on 23rd February to Rotterdam for modifications. Renamed *Kimolos* and rebuilt at Perama where her accommodation was extended both fore and aft.

1981

On 24th November the ship grounded at Sifnos and retired to Piraeus for repairs.

1983

Ship grounded at Sifnos again on 17th June but this time on sand and she was able to refloat herself. On 28th September the ship hit the breakwater at Syros bringing down the lighthouse,

The *Kallisti* arrives at Santorini in September 2001. *(Miles Cowsill)*

bending her screws and partially flooding her engine room. Refloated herself later in the day and dry-docked at Piraeus on 3rd October.

1992

On 21st October the ship ran aground off Rhodes, passengers were evacuated and the vessel was refloated ten days later.

1993

At midnight on 25th February the ship ran aground in Kamares Bay on the island of Sifnos in heavy weather. Passengers were evacuated and the ship was refloated two days later.

1993

Renamed *Ergina*.

1995

Renamed *Methodia II*. Arrested on 13th July.

1996

Laid-up and sold by public auction in Greece on 1st March but later seized by authorities.

The **Kallisti** arrives at Heraklion following one of her daily cruises to Santorini. *(John May)*

1997

Renamed *Kallisti* - owners Saronic Cruises SA. Operating summer day cruises (no cars) from Heraklion (Crete) to the volcanic island of Santorini..

2002

Offered for sale.

Free Enterprise II

This vessel was the first British-registered drive-through car ferry and was certainly the shape of things to come. Since the construction of the *Free Enterprise* three years earlier, the anticipated freight growth had failed to materialise and so the new ship's vehicle deck headroom was lowered to 11 ft. 2 ins. This was very soon to become her Achilles heel once the new trade developed but the ship was ideal for the summer tourist trade with cars and caravans. She was therefore the least successful of the eight 'Free Enterprise' ships and Roland Wickenden announced at the

The launch of the *Free Enterprise II* on 29th January 1965. *(John Hendy's collection)*

launch of the *Free Enterprise IV* in March 1969 that she was to be offered for sale with a delivery date at the same time as the entry into service of the *Free Enterprise V* in May 1970.

1965

Ship launched at Schiedam on 29th January by Mrs. Bernice Nott. On 9th May she arrived at Dover at 09.00. 19th May - Special early morning trip from Calais to Dover with Munich football supporters before her press trip to Calais when the ship opened the port's second linkspan at berth 4. George Nott was made a Freeman of Calais. On 22nd May at 10.30 the maiden commercial voyage to Calais (Captain David Bruce). At 4,011 gross tons the £1.3 million ship was the largest car ferry in the English Channel.

An artist's impression of the *Free Enterprise II* as illustrated in the 1964 brochure. *(Ferry Publications Library)*

A bow view of the **Free Enterprise II** berthing at Dover's Prince of Wales' Pier following her maiden voyage on 22nd May 1965. Captain David Bruce is on the port bridge wing. *(John Hendy)*

1966

17th March - Opened the new service from Dover (12.00) to Zeebrugge using the original floating pontoon berth (registered as *Auto-Carrier*) at the entrance to the Baudouin Canal.

1967

The *Free Enterprise III* took over the Zeebrugge runs in January leaving the first two ships on the Calais service.

1969

The British Railways Board (later Sealink) looked at the ship when she was offered for sale during August. During the winter she was laid up at Bruges.

1970

Ship laid-up in the Wellington Dock at Dover before operating a summer season (18th June - 20th September) on the Southampton - Cherbourg link. She was used on a 12.30 sailing from Southampton with an 18.30 return with an additional trip on Fridays, Saturdays and Sundays.

Trials at Southampton on 2nd February after which these were repeated at Cherbourg. Ship then sailed for overhaul at Amsterdam before berthing in Dover's Wellington Dock. Berth congestion at Calais over the Easter weekend saw the ship sail to Boulogne on 27th March - the first Townsend ship to dock there. Ship sailed to Southampton on 4th June. Started Cherbourg crossings with 12.30 on 18th June. Sprung a leak on 14th July and was dry-docked at Southampton. On 25th July, on the 12.30 to Cherbourg, there was an engine room explosion 22 miles off Cherbourg. A cylinder lining

The *Free Enterprise II* arrives at Dover on her return maiden voyage on 22nd May 1965. *(John Hendy)*

Left: The *Free Enterprise II* arriving at Dover. *(John Hendy)*

TOWNSEND DOVER/CALAIS
the shortest way to the Continent

TOWNSEND FERRIES have trebled car carrying capacity for 1966
and can now take passengers without vehicles

the only independent cross-Channel ferry line...
reliability that only 38 years experience can give

TOWNSEND DRIVE-IN/DRIVE-THROUGH CAR FERRIES
the lowest cost way to the Continent

FREE ENTERPRISE II

Press Sailing

19th MAY 1965

DOVER-CALAIS

TOWNSEND CAR FERRIES LTD.

The *Free Enterprise II* leaves the Eastern Arm at Dover to take up the morning sailing to Calais. *(Miles Cowsill)*

Above: The *Free Enterprise II* in the lock at Zeebrugge in October 1966. *(John Hendy)*
Below: The *Free Enterprise II* at Newhaven during her charter to Sealink for the Dieppe route in 1980. Note that the Townsend Thoresen logo has been painted over. *(John May)*

had disintigrated, jamming a piston which caused the starboard engine to seize and explode. Due to bad weather rescue boats did not reach her until 21.25 and she was towed into Cherbourg at 03.30 the following morning. Ship sailed to Rotterdam on one engine on 28th July and returned to service on 8th August. At the end of her seasonal service, the ship was laid-up at Zeebrugge from 22nd September. She was later moved up the canal to Bruges.

1971

Arrived back at Southampton from Zeebrugge on 30th April. Southampton - Cherbourg again between 21st May and 19th September. Two daily services: 12.30 and 00.30.

9th August - ship in King George V Graving Dock with propeller problems. On completing her service she sailed to Le

Havre where she made a successful fit with the linkspan on 23rd September. She then left for the Dover - Zeebrugge link where she relieved Thoresen's freighter *Viking IV*. The spare ship found useful winter employment when she was chartered by the 'Evening News' to act as the venue for a motor racing car show in the Pool of London. The charter lasted from 31st December until 9th January 1972. Winter lay-up at Bruges for a third year.

1973

Arrived at Southampton from Dover on 11th May for the seasonal Cherbourg service which commenced on 18th May.

1974

The ship again became the base for a floating racing car show in the Pool of London. She arrived on 3rd January and was open between 5th-20th January. She discharged her cars at Dover before sailing to the Ocean Dock at Southampton to lay-up. A brief return to Dover was necessary when on 5th April the *Free Enterprise V* damaged her stern while berthing. Then Southampton - Cherbourg between 27th June and 15th September - a shorter season than usual. This was her final season at Southampton.

1979

During the summer, the first three 'Free Enterprises' operated

The ***Free Enterprise II*** arrives at Calais during her final spell on the service in 1980. *(John Hendy)*

to Calais together for one final time before the *Free Enterprise II* laid-up again at Tilbury on 3rd September.

1980

Final service on the Dover - Calais route during April and May with the new *Spirit of Free Enterprise* and the *Free Enterprise VIII*. Then lay-up at Le Havre. 9th May - on charter to Sealink UK Ltd for service between Weymouth - Channel Islands and Portsmouth

Above: The *Free Enterprise II* off Bembridge, Isle of Wight outward bound from Portsmouth to Cherbourg whilst operating on the Western Channel services. *(John Hendy)*

Left: This view shows the *Free Enterprise II* with the *Free Enterprise III*, laid up at Southampton pending their disposal from the fleet. *(Miles Cowsill)*

- Channel Islands. Ran two trips from Portsmouth on 10th - 11th May but inability to carry freight affected her operational use. Thereafter switched to run from Weymouth between 21st May - 11th June. On 18th June on charter on the Newhaven - Dieppe (13.00 and 20.00 return) route vice the *Senlac* which was off service after fire damage. Then Portsmouth - Cherbourg for the summer season in company with the *Viking Victory*. On 17th August, to the strains of "Land of Hope and Glory" over the ship's tannoy, the ship (with Captain Mike Edward in command) ran and

beat the fishermens' blockade at Cherbourg. Thereafter the company adopted a new slogan - "The fleet you can't beat!"

The *Moby Blu* (ex *Free Enterprise II*) arrives at Piombino in July 1997. *(Frank Heine)*

1981

Ship laid-up for sale at Southampton. During May her bell was presented to the Port of Zeebrugge by Keith Wickenden to celebrate the fifteen year link.

1982

End of September a deposit paid for the ship and on 14th October she left Southampton as the *Moby Blu*. New Italian owners - Navigazione Arcipelago Maddalino SPA of Caligari, Sardinia - usually known as NavArMa (later Moby Lines). During her recent career with Moby she has mainly worked the 60 minute service linking Piombino (Italy) and Portoferrairo (Elba) but was offered for sale for $1 million in 2001.

2002 -

In service from mid-June.

The *Free Enterprise III* leaving Dover for Calais for her official trials before entering service in July 1996. *(John Hendy)*

Free Enterprise III

The £2 million *Free Enterprise III* was a transitional ship and had she been built 18 months later then she would have, in all probability, been a totally different vessel. She was built to carry either 221 cars or 14 pieces of freight (on her wing decks) with 102 cars. With freight demanding even more space and the size and weight of lorries increasing, the crews struggled to load her frequently using wooden wedges and soapy water to slide heavy wheels into position in the freight alleys. Her first Master, Captain Jack Dawson wrote of her, "We all felt that with slightly different dimensions, the FEIII was the ideal ro-ro ship of the future." PR material claimed that the ship was three years ahead of her time. As with the the FE II, the FE III was fitted with the unsuccessful flume stabiliser system.

1965
Keel laid - 23rd November.

1966
Vessel launched at Schiedam on 14th May 1966 by Mrs. Josephine Wickenden, wife of the new Managing Director of George Nott Industries, Mr. Roland Wickenden. 21st July - ship arrived at Dover Eastern Docks (berth 4) at 10.30 flying the IHC flag and Dutch tricolour. Ship entered service a week early completing her maiden voyage (Captain Jack Dawson) on 22nd July. Left Dover at 13.30 for trials at Calais and first commercial

Above: The *Free Enterprise III* on the stocks prior to her launch in May 1966. *(John Hendy's collection)*

Below: The *Free Enterprise III* seen shortly after her launch and being manoeuvred to her fitting-out berth. *(John Hendy's collection)*

voyage at 21.15 the same day. The vessel took less than six months to build. On 4th October the ship returned to Schiedam for the part removal and repositioning of the insulation around the funnel uptakes.

1967

Transferred to the Dover - Zeebrugge link on 15th January and 'inaugural' trip on 1st February. The ship brought a 20% increase in freight capacity on the route. During early May she was on refit when the *Free Enterprise II* deputised on the Zeebrugge link.

1968

During mid-November a lorry carrying liquid nitrogen spilled some of its contents onto the ship's vehicle deck causing considerable damage to the deck and cross-beams. The ship returned to Zeebrugge and discharged her cargo at the train ferry berth before sailing for repairs. During this period off service she had her Quiet Lounge added to her Bridge Deck (immediately forward of the funnel). The ship was off service for almost a month during which time Thoresen's *Viking II* deputised.

1970

With the arrival on station of the *Free Enterprise V* on 31st

Dover Zeebrugge
Dover Calais

Townsend
Car-Way to your Continent sunshine

Above: A stern view of the *Free Enterprise III* outward bound from Dover to Calais for trials in July 1966. *(John Hendy)*
Below: The main lounge area onboard the *Free Enterprise III*. *(John Hendy)*

May, the FE III was displaced on the Zeebrugge service and returned to run the summer Calais link.

1971

16th March - minor engine room explosion on board during an evening Calais - Dover sailing. With the FE V off service between 11th-13th October the vessel was switched from the Calais route to deputise. On 27th December the ship picked up the crew of the small coastal tug *En Avant* which had foundered off the Varne light during her delivery voyage.

The *Free Enterprise III* is seen leaving Calais for Dover in August 1979. *(Bernard McCall)*

1972

Maintaining the Dover - Calais summer service with the *Free Enterprise I*.

1973

Summer: Dover - Calais service. During overhauls, the ship returned to the Belgian service and suffered engine problems on 17th December when the *Free Enterprise I* deputised on the Zeebrugge link.

1974

With the *Free Enterprise VIII* in service, the FE III became spare and so was transferred to the new Cairnryan - Larne link. Trials were carried out on 29th June and she commenced service as from 1st July working the 08.15, 13.15 and 18.30 from Larne with the 10.45, 15.45 and 21.00 returns. Her 1 hour 45 minute schedules proved to be too tight. The season closed on 19th October. On 21st October the ship replaced the FE I on the Calais link allowing the smaller ship to lay-up.

1975

Summer: Dover - Calais service.

1977

During March the ship was overhauled by British Rail in Dover's Granville Dock before summer service on Dover - Calais.

1978

Summer service: Dover - Calais.

Special sailing in July to celebrate the company's 50 years of operation.

Above: An interesting summer view of the *Free Enterprise III* at berth 4 with the *Lord Warden* in the foreground pending her 11.30 departure to Boulogne. *(John Hendy's collection)*

Below: The *Free Enterprise III* arrives at Cairnryan for the first time from Larne on 1st July 1974. *(Paul Clegg)*

The *Free Enterprise III* coming astern at Larne in July 1974. *(Paul Clegg)*

1979

Overhaul in the Granville Dock at Dover was repeated between 27th February - 15th March.

1980

On Dover - Calais with the *Spirit of Free Enterprise* and *Herald of Free Enterprise*. With the imminent arrival of the *Pride of Free Enterprise*, the ship finished service at Dover on 31st October when she was destored after which she sailed to Le Havre for lay-up.

1981

In June the spare *Free Enterprise III* was chartered by Sealink UK Ltd. for service on their Dover - Calais/ Boulogne seasonal rail-connected links vice the *Caledonian Princess*. Ship arrived at Dover on 24th June and took up service from Calais - Dover Western Docks at 09.55 the next morning also offering the 13.00 to Boulogne. She broke down twice and was off service with stabiliser problems during first week of service. Whilst laying alongisde the Admiralty Pier on 3rd July, the ship was hit by the French train ferry *Saint Eloi* as a result of which she missed a sailing. Sailed from Dover 22.00 on 10th July to become the seasonal Portsmouth - Cherbourg link with the *Viking Victory* working the 07.00 and 18.15 from Portsmouth between 16th July - 6th September.

1982

Townsend Thoresen found themselves short of freight ships during the Falklands War and with the *Europic Ferry* requisitioned

Above: The *Free Enterprise III* arriving at Portsmouth from Cherbourg in August 1981. *(Miles Cowsill)*

Below: This view shows the *Free Enterprise III* laid up in Southampton's Empress Dock awaiting disposal. *(Miles Cowsill)*

and before the *Gaelic Ferry* could transfer from Felixstowe, from 6th May the FE III was recommissioned to work passenger sailings from Portsmouth - Cherbourg - Southampton. At 19.00 on 10th May some 18 miles south of the Isle of Wight an engine room explosion (caused by a piston failure in the port engine) caused the ship to lose power and seriously injured two members of the engine room staff. With HMS *Southampton* standing by, the ship drifted down Channel and eventually reached Southampton at 07.00 the following day. The ship was repaired and laid-up in Southampton later being joined there by the *Free Enterprise II*.

1983

The ship was used between 10th - 17th January on freight sailings which proved unsatisfactory. Laid-up in the Ocean Dock followed by the Empress Dock.

1984

Sold in late July to Mira Shipping Line of Malta (owned by Mr. George Zammit and purchased for service to north Africa), renamed *Tamira* but never used by the company. Left Empress Dock, Southampton on 24th August and arrived Valletta on 2nd September. On 26th October the ship was sold to Isle of Man Steam Packet Co. for £600,000 and renamed *Mona's Isle* (VI). Left 6th December for refit at Clydebank Engineering at Govan arriving on 13th December under the command of Captain Vernon Kinley.

1985

Arrived Douglas 3rd April. Sailed 'light ship' to Dun

The **Mona's Isle** in the Lune Channel off Heysham in September 1985 during her brief and unsuccessful career with the Isle of Man Steam Packet Company. *(John Hendy)*

Laoghaire on 4th April returning at 02.00 the following day. Returned to Govan for modifications to ramp 17th-20th April. Took up Douglas - Heysham on 21st April. 22nd July - aground at Heysham. Severe operational problems resulting from the extra weight added during her refit meant that she could only carry 200 tonnes before she was down 'on her marks.' Final sailing to Heysham on 4th October and laid-up for sale at Birkenhead (arrived 7th October).

1986

March 25th - Sold to Eygptian company Sadaka Shipping Lines of Suez and renamed *Al Fahad*. Left 7th April.

1990

On a voyage between Suez (Egypt) and Jeddah (Saudi Arabia) on 16th November the vessel lost her rudder and fouled a propeller. Taken in tow to Suez where repairs were completed by 16th December.

1992

20th December - On voyage between Suez and Jeddah she collided with the ferry *Mecca I* while berthed at Port Ibrahim, Suez. Damage to starboard side promenade deck but sailed the same day.

1998

Ship laid-up at Suez and does not appear to have been used since summer that year.

The ***Al Fahad*** at Jeddah, Saudi Arabia. *(Frank Heine)*

Free Enterprise IV

The *Free Enterprise IV* was the ship that established the Zeebrugge route as a major player in the cross-Channel arena. Townsends had experienced a tremendous degree of hostility from the Belgian Government over the construction of a purpose-built terminal at the Belgian port. It should be remembered at this time that their Dover - Ostend ferries carried 80% of the UK - Belgium traffic and were reluctant to allow

The *Free Enterprise IV* in her first season outward bound from Dover to Zeebrugge on her morning sailing to Belgium. *(John Hendy)*

Townsend see through their ambitious expansion plans. Roland Wickenden announced that the decision to build a *Free Enterprise IV* very much depended on a change of attitude from the Belgian Government. This was fortunately forthcoming and it was the 'FE IV' that had the honour of officially opening the new £300,000 facilities at the foot of the mole on 1st April 1972. The FE IV was the first of the series to adopt the triple-screw/ single rudder arrangement which the other four ships followed.

1969

On 1st March, launched at Schiedam by Mrs. Kitty Bradford, wife of a Director. Arrived at Dover on 28th May and undertook trials on the following day. 1st June - maiden voyage to Zeebrugge under the command of Captain Jack Dawson.

1970

On 4th January the ship undertook berthing trials in Southampton's Princess Alexandra Dock later sailing to Amsterdam for drydocking.

The AA's 'Drive' magazine wrote of the ship: "Launched only recently, the ship has a touch of the luxury liner about it. The appointments are comfortable with small artificial flower arrangements and pretty porthole curtains."

1972

1st April - At 10.00 she officially opened the new Zeebrugge car ferry terminal at the shore end of the mole. Following the eventual entry into service of the *Free Enterprise VI* the ship was moved to the 09.00 and 21.00 sailings from Dover.

This splendid view shows the *Free Enterprise IV* arriving at Dover for the first time from the builders. Notice that the *Free Enterprise I* is at berth 4 loading for Calais. *(FotoFlite)*

1973

Ship on summer Calais services with the FE I and FE III.

1974

After the entry into service of the *Free Enterprise VIII* on 18th July, the ship was moved to the 05.35 and 17.35 cycle from Dover to Zeebrugge.

1976

After two loss-making seasons, the ship became the third attempt to find the right vessel for the Cairnryan - Larne route which she commenced on 20th May. Local unions had feared the loss of jobs and rivals Sealink had plans for a third ship on their rival Larne - Stranraer service. It was announced before Christmas

The *Free Enterprise IV* leaving Calais in June 1975 in her intermediate Townsend Thoresen livery of dark green.
(Andrew Jones)

1975 that the FE IV would run the service. A vigorous marketing campaign saw the service become a success and she remained on the North Channel until 1986. On her first day in service, under the command of Captain George Kayne, she crossed to Larne in 1 hour 41 minutes - a new record. At the end of the season (sailing in tandem with the *Doric Ferry*) she returned to Dover for the winter.

1977

North Channel season lasted from 6th April -2nd October and from 30th October - 31st December.

The *Free Enterprise IV* pictured in Loch Ryan at speed outward bound from Cairnryan to Larne. *(Harry Cathcart)*

The *Free Enterprise IV* and *European Enterprise* in the Camber at Dover in 1986. *(John Hendy)*

1982

The recession coupled with the fall off in traffic to Northern Ireland saw plan to lay ship up in Barrow during the summer season but retained following representations from the NUS. Following her Tyne refit, on 18th February she sailed to Felixstowe to take up the Zeebrugge route where she deputised for the regular ships *Viking Viscount* and *Viking Voyager*. Returned to the North Channel for Easter sailings.

1983

Following overhaul on the Tyne in February, the ship sailed again for the Felixstowe - Zeebrugge link.

1984

Hurricane force winds in the North Channel on 14th January saw the ship break her moorings at Cairnryan and sustain hull damage following contact with a dolphin. Sailed to Larne and continued to service until Tyne refit on 29th January. On completion, she again sailed for the Felixstowe - Zeebrugge link finishing on 28th March.

1985

January dry-docking at Govan after which she again sailed to Felixstowe.

1986

Final stint at Felixstowe from end March - end May then back to Cairnryan to await the transfer of the *Dragon* from Portsmouth. The ship left Larne for the final time on 10th July

the townsend eight

arriving at Dover on 13th July and after repairs to her bow-thrust unit at Dunkirk, refitted in the Granville Dock at Dover from 15th July. Waiter-service restaurant became a self-service cafeteria, the passenger cabins were gutted and fitted with reclinable seating while the main lounge was also extensively refurbished. Left the Granville Dock at midnight on 1st August and stored at the disused number 1 berth at Dover Eastern Docks. She entered service on the Boulogne route with the 09.30 on 3rd August replacing the former P&O Normandy Ferries vessel *nf Panther*. The service normally used number 2 at Dover (bow in) and number 15 at Boulogne where the double-deck linkspan was utilised.

The former the *Free Enterprise IV* is seen here as the *Falster Link* arriving at Travemunde with a red hull. Notice the bow modification. *(Ulrich Streich)*

1987.

At 00.38 on 26th October the ship was the last vessel to leave the original Camber berths before the area was reclaimed. The ship was not renamed at the formation of P&O European Ferries in October as she was so close to retirement. On the morning of 4th December she was replaced in the fleet by the *Pride of Calais* and after her final arrival from Boulogne that morning de-stored at berth 1 prior to lay-up pending sale at Chatham. Her Boulogne roster was taken by the *Pride of Canterbury* (ex *Free Enterprise VIII*) which had arrived from Zeebrugge for the final time that morning.

1988

During January the ship was reactivated to take the place of

An unusual view of the *Free Enterprise IV* turning off the berth at Felixstowe on 9th March 1985 while on the Zeebrugge service. *(Miles Cowsill)*

the damaged *Pride of Canterbury* but only ran the Dover-Boulogne service for a brief period before the start of the NUS strike after which she returned to Chatham to lay-up. In April the ship was sold to Danish owners and renamed *Falster Link* (Bahamian flag) for GT Link (later Europa Linien) for service linking Gedser (Denmark) with Travemunde (West Germany) and following reunification, Rostock (Germany).

1994

On 28th June a fire started in a lorry just after the ship had left Gedser. The ship lost all steering and power and was forced to

The *Tag Al Salam* (ex *Free Enterprise IV*) pictured at Suez in May 1998 following conversion work for service work between Egypt and Saudi Arabia. *(Frank Heine)*

anchor 3 miles off the Danish port. Fire extinguished and the vessel towed back to Gedser. Repairs at Nakskov.

1998

During April ship sold to the Egyptian company El Salam Shipping Co. and renamed *Tag Al Salam* - meaning Crown of Peace - (Panamanian flag) and joining the former FE VI. During May she commenced service linking Port Safaga (Egypt) with Duba (Saudi Arabia) in the Red Sea.

The blue-hulled *Falster Link* seen in the Europa Linien livery arriving at Gedser. Sponsons have been added to the vessel. *(Frank Lose)*

Free Enterprise V
Pride of Hythe

Such was the success of the *Free Enterprise IV* and the flourishing new service to Belgium that her design became the 'standard' for the company's short-sea crossings. New ships with greater freight capacity were placed on the Zeebrugge service while the older units dropped back to maintain the Calais schedules. She was downgraded in the summer of 1982, when she was sent to work the Portsmouth-Cherbourg, link but returned to Dover during the period when the *Free Enterprise VI* and *Free Enterprise VII* were being stretched. The acquisition of the P&O Normandy Ferries service to Boulogne in 1985 undoubtedly prolonged her career in the Dover-based fleet.

The ***Free Enterprise V*** following her launch in May 1968. *(John Hendy's collection)*

1970
Launched 31st January at Schiedam by Mrs. Jane Thompson wife of a Director. The £2.5 million vessel arrived in Dover on 23rd May. On 27th May the ship undertook a special sailing to Zeebrugge with army personnel and returned full of freight. 31st May - maiden commercial voyage from Dover to Zeebrugge (Captain Jack Dawson).

1971
Out of service for three days (11th-13th October) when the FE III took her place on the Zeebrugge link. On 20th November the ship was blown against the submarine pens whilst berthing at the Eastern Docks in a force 11. She was out of service the next day.

1972
On 22nd December the ship collided with the British coaster *Redthorne* off Zeebrugge. Sailed to Antwerp for repairs when the FE III covered for her while the FE I was brought out of winter lay-up to deputise on the Calais link.

1973
Back from repairs on 6th January. Operating the Zeebrugge service with her two later sisters.

The *Free Enterprise V* approaching St. Margaret's Bay and the South Foreland during her early career on the Zeebrugge service. *(FotoFlite)*

1974

Ship sustained major stern damage when berthing at Dover on 5th April. To Vlissingen for repairs. Replaced in service by the FE II. On entry into service of the *Free Enterprise VIII* on 17th July, the ship was transferred to the Calais link for the summer season.

1975

The last four 'Free Enterprises' on the summer Zeebrugge link.

1977

The ship spent the summer period on the Calais service with the first three 'Free Enterprises.'

The *Free Enterprise V* at berth 4 at Dover pending her departure to Zeebrugge. *(John Hendy)*

A morning view of the *Free Enterprise V* as she arrives at Zeebrugge from Dover. *(Mike Louagie)*

1978

Summer ship rosters repeated from 1977.

1981

The recession coupled with a £9.23 million loss during the first six months of the year saw the ship withdrawn from the Dover - Zeebrugge link following her 17.30 sailing on 27th September. She returned at 01.00 on the following morning and was not expected to sail again from Dover.

1982

Early in the year saw the ship laid up in the King George V Dock in London before sailing to Southampton to run extra freight

Possibly the livery by which many will remember the Townsend Thoresen fleet. This view shows the *Free Enterprise V* with her orange hull and TTF livery introduced in 1976. (FotoFlite)

sailings to Le Havre (departing 07.00 and returning at 23.00) in company with the *Europic Ferry*. Switched to the Portsmouth - Cherbourg summer season from 20th May replacing the *Viking Victory*. Returned to Southampton to run extra freight sailings when summer season closed at end of September.

1983

The ship returned to Dover late in the year to cover freight sailings of the *Free Enterprise VIII* which sailed to Amsterdam for the uprating of her passenger accommodation.

1984

Final Portsmouth - Cherbourg summer season after which the ship sailed to Dover for winter Zeebrugge reliefs (running with a passenger certificate for 132).

1985

On 30th March the ship sailed to Chatham for refit. While the *nf Tiger* and *nf Panther* were away at Immingham receiving the Townsend Thoresen livery, the ship stood in on the Boulogne run starting with the 18.00 sailing on 9th April.

In June the ship transferred to Dover - Zeebrugge to cover jumboisation periods of firstly the *Free Enterprise VI* and then *Free Enterprise VII*.

The *Free Enterprise V* in the Swashway inward bound to Portsmouth from Cherbourg in 1984. *(John Hendy)*

The *Free Enterprise V* outward bound from Dover sporting the new livery introduced in 1974 with the larger Townsend Thoresen wording and dark green hull. *(FotoFlite)*

In 1984 Townsend Thoresen introduced a further livery modification incorporating a white TT to the funnels of their ships. This picture shows the **Free Enterprise V**. *(Mike Louagie)*

1986

Ship returned from overhaul on 11th January and took up sailings to Boulogne vice the *nf Tiger* which went off for a five day refit. The *Spirit of Free Enterprise* ran the ship's Zeebrugge schedules at this time. With the return from stretching of the FE VII in March, the ship was switched to Portsmouth - Le Havre until replaced there by the *Viking Viscount* from Felixstowe on 7th May after which the FE V laid-up at Southampton. With the departure

of the *Dragon* for Scotland on 10th June prior to taking up the Larne - Cairnryan route (as the *Ionic Ferry*), the ship was reactivated and returned to Portsmouth until the stretched *Viking Valiant* returned to service.

Took up the Dover - Boulogne service vice the former P&O Normandy Ferries vessel *nf Tiger* with the 18.30 sailing on 18th July.

1987

The loss of the *Herald of Free Enterprise* off Zeebrugge on 6th March saw Townsend Thoresen charter the spare Sealink ship

An afternoon view of the **Pride of Hythe** arriving at Boulogne from Dover in 1989. *(John Hendy)*

The **Pride of Hythe** leaving Boulogne in October 1990. *(Mike Louagie)*

Vortigern for 60 days as from 1st April. The FE V was therefore freed from Boulogne and switched to Calais sailings (vice the 'Herald') but was replaced by the new *Pride of Dover* as from 2nd June. With the formation of P&O European Ferries in October the ship was renamed *Pride of Hythe*..

1988

During the ship's refit (from 13th January), the ship's services on the Boulogne link were taken by the freighter *European Endeavour* running at 06.30, 12.30 and 18.30 from Dover. The NUS strike commenced in late January and Boulogne sailings were suspended until 19th August. During April she was offered for sale. The 'Hythe' restarted service in early September.

1992

After her return from a Bremerhaven refit the ship took up the 04.45 Dover - Boulogne on 30th March allowing the *Pride of Walmer* (ex FE VII) to stand-down for two days while work was carried out on her Club Class lounge. On 1st April the ship was transferred to the Dover - Calais route to await the arrival of the stretched *Pride of Kent* (ex *Spirit of Free Enterprise*). Due to delays, the ship returned to the Boulogne service (vice the *Pride of Walmer*, (ex FE VII) on 5th June.

1993
The Dover - Boulogne route was closed 'with immediate effect' on 4th January - eight years to the day since the European Ferries Group had purchased P&O Normandy Ferries for £12.5 million. The ship was sent to Tilbury and offered for sale. In June she was renamed *Laburnum* (Cypriot flag) after her sale to Charter Hall Shipping Co. of Limassol, a subsidiary of the Slovenian company TransEuropa Shipping Lines (Denval Ltd) for a 10 hour service

The former *Free Enterprise V* seen as the *Laburnum* at the port of Bari whilst the vessel was employed on a cross Adriatic service between Italy and Montenegro. *(John May)*

The *Laburnum* arrives at Ostend from Ramsgate in March 2002. *(Miles Cowsill)*

across the Adriatic Sea linking Bari (Italy) and Bar (Montenegro). Ship sailed for remedial work in Dunkirk.

2001
Adriatic service suspended and on 13th July the largely unaltered *Laburnum* arrived at Ostend to take up the company's freight service to Ramsgate.

Free Enterprise VI
Pride of Sandwich
Pride of Ailsa

In December 1970 Townsend Thoresen announced a five ship building programme. Two ships were destined for Dover - the *Free Enterprise VI*, which was due for delivery on 15th April 1972, and the *Free Enterprise VII* which was due in February 1973.

Although looking almost identical to the previous two ships of the series, the FE VI was the first to receive three important modifications. Her interior platform decks allowed her to carry 314 cars as opposed to the 260 in the earlier vessels of the series, mechanically she was fitted with the more powerful Stork-Werkspoor engines rather than the Smit-MAN engines of the previous ships and she was the first of the series to receive fin stabilisers.

1972

Launched at Schiedam on 29th January by Mrs. Joan Ayres, wife of Director and Group Naval Architect James Ayres. Maiden voyage to Zeebrugge due on 15th June but the ship arrived late on the day after. She was promptly returned to the builders with a fault in her exhaust system concerning the bellows which kept cracking and leaking gasses. Being a ship short, Townsend chartered the Sealink car ferry *Normannia* for the Calais service until 26th June. Maiden voyage to Zeebrugge on about 30th June (Captain Jack Dawson) and to Calais on about 8th July. Ship used on 21.00 to Zeebrugge and two daytime sailings to Calais (09.00 and 15.00).

1973

Without the required berthing slots available at Calais for extra weekend sailings, Townsend turned to Boulogne and operated 30 extra Friday and Saturday sailings during the peak season. These were operated in place of two round Zeebrugge trips.

1974

The *Free Enterprise VI* repeated the previous season's Boulogne sailings operating on Saturdays and Sundays between 6th July - 8th September. Not repeated in 1975.

1976

During early May Commodore Dawson finally lowered his flag and retired from the fleet. Although his final ship was the FE VIII, press photographs were taken of the Commodore's flag being lowered on the FE VI.

1978

On 8th May, the ship struck the East Pier at Calais and was holed amidships flooding part of the engine room. She returned to port, where she discharged passengers, before sailing to Rotterdam for dry-docking, repairs and re-wiring.

the Townsend eight

Arriving at Dover from Zeebrugge on 9th June 1981, the *Free Enterprise VI* is captured at the moment her screws are turned ahead in order to slow her way. *(John Hendy)*

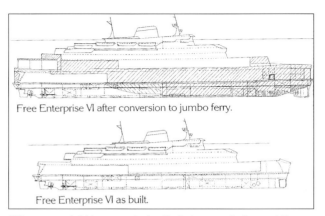

Free Enterprise VI after conversion to jumbo ferry.

Free Enterprise VI as built.

With even more freight space required on the Zeebrugge route, Townsend Thoresen decided to spend £45 million rebuilding the *Free Enterprise VI* and *Free Enterprise VII*.

Four mammoth floating cranes were used to lift the vessels' original superstructures which were then deposited on the quayside to await the new hulls.(*Ferry Publications Library*)

1985

June - Ship sent to Schichau Unterweser AG (SUAG) at Bremerhaven for rebuilding. The 1,260 ton superstructure was lifted off by four mammoth cranes. The bow section of the vessel was removed and a new forward hull section was added. The keel for the new fore-bodies (also that of the *Free Enterprise VII* - yard numbers 2289 and 2290) was laid in January and was launched on 18th May by Margaret Ayres and Lauren Siddle whose mothers had launched the original ships. Measuring 135 metres x 22 metres, the two new bow sections were cut into two and welded onto the forward end of the original hulls before the superstructures were replaced. The work increased lorry capacity from 24 to 60. The ship arrived back at Dover on 26th October and following trials at

The *Free Enterprise VI* following her conversion. This 1987 view shows the vessel sporting the pale blue P&O funnel. *(John Hendy)*

The *Pride of Sandwich* coming astern at Zeebrugge following completion of another four hour run between Dover and the Belgian port. *(Mike Louagie)*

Calais two days later, re-entered service with the 20.30 Dover - Zeebrugge. Provided additional Calais services during the busy approach to Christmas.

1987

With the formation of P&O European Ferries in October the ship was renamed *Pride of Sandwich*.

1991

On 31st December the Zeebrugge service was closed to passengers. With the Channel Tunnel about to be opened, it had been decided that all such traffic would in future be funnelled through Dover - Calais via the company's new 'shuttle' service. The move also assisted P&O's operating partners RMT who then

The *Pride of Sandwich* (ex *Free Enterprise VI*) is pictured following the application of the dark blue P&O livery. The ship is seen approaching Zeebrugge in April 1989. *(Mike Louagie)*

the **Townsend** eight

The **Pride of Sandwich** nearing Zeebrugge in April 1989. *(John Hendy)*

maintained the Ostend - Dover link.

1992

The *Pride of Sandwich* continued on her previous schedules in a freight mode until 3rd January before finishing with the 23.45 from Dover and the 06.45 return after which the new freighter *European Pathway* took up the link with the 11.45 from Dover. The ship then sailed to Chatham for the fitting of a temporary stern-ramp before relieving on the Felixstowe - Zeebrugge link. Sailed to Falmouth for modifications and refit (arrived 28th February), and

The **Pride of Al Salam 95** (ex **Pride of Ailsa**) sails from Suez in May 1998. *(Frank Heine)*

renamed *Pride of Ailsa* on 5th March. Work carried out included the removal of her hoistable car decks to give maximum height for freight, the removal of the Dover skywalk and cutting of a new passenger access point on E Deck, new stern arrangements for Larne, the refurbishment of the Club Class lounge behind the funnel and a new children's play area in place of the original perfume shop. The ship left Falmouth on 12th March and arrived at Larne for trials on 13th March before sailing to Cairnryan to take up the 15.30 sailing.

1993

On 5th August the ship sustained engine damage after which repairs were completed at Belfast.

1996

On 15th June (under the command of Captain Eddie Irvine) the ship operated her final sailings before being replaced in the fleet by the fast craft *Jetliner*. Missing the 08.00 from Larne (due to rudder problems), she worked the 15.30 to Cairnryan and 19.30 (retarded to 20.00) return. After discharging she sailed at midnight for Belfast. Ship handed over to her new Egyptian owners El Salam Shipping Co. on 17th June leaving for Port Said five days later. Renamed *Pride of Al Salam 95* (Panamanian flag) for 40 hour

Not a happy sight. Further conversion work was undertaken to the former **Free Enterprise VI**, prior to her entering service from Suez. This view shows the extensive passenger areas added to the vessel aft following her disposal by P&O. The upper lorry deck was converted into two decks of cabins. *(Frank Heine)*

service in the Red Sea carrying pilgrims between Egypt and Saudi Arabia. Her upper vehicle deck was converted to cabin use and the passenger certificate raised from 610 to as many as 2,500.

(note: It is of interest that the former Dover-based Townsend Thoresen freighter *European Trader* also passed to this company during late 2001).

Free Enterprise VII
Pride of Walmer
Pride of Rathlin

Ordered at the same time as the *Free Enterprise VI* (whose career she closely mirrored) there was an obvious exterior difference with the mainmast resited further aft and not on the roof of the after deck house. This modification (for navigational reasons) was continued with the *Free Enterprise VIII*. Another modification concerned her inward turning propellers which proved so successful that the FE VIII and all subsequent vessels were similarly treated. Both the centre and port screws were right turning while the starboard propeller was left turning. This produced a paddle wheel effect which greatly improved their handling.

1972

Ship launched at Schiedam on 21st October by Mrs. Ann Siddle, the wife of Director (and future Managing Director) Kenneth Siddle. Tragically the Group's inspirational Managing Director Roland Wickenden died on the train to Zeebrugge during his return to England.

The *Free Enterprise VII* at Dover berth 4 prior to a departure for Zeebrugge. *(John May)*

The *Free Enterprise VII* comes astern at Dover. *(John May)*

The *Free Enterprise VII* pictured during her first season in service between Dover and Zeebrugge. *(Miles Cowsill)*

1973

Ship delivered on 23rd February. Maiden voyage to Zeebrugge on 26th February (Captain Jack Dawson).

1985

In order to accommodate extra freight, the ship was rebuilt at SUAG Bremerhaven between November 1985 - March 1986. (The modifications are described in the *Free Enterprise VI* section but affected neither ship's passenger accommodation).

1986

On 9th March the ship re-entered service on the Dover - Zeebrugge link.

The fore-bodies of the *Free Enterprise VI* and *Free Enterprise VII* were laid down in January 1985 and launched in the following May. The *Free Enterprise VII* re-entered service on 9th March 1986. *(Ferry Publications Library)*

The jumboised *Free Enterprise VII* inward bound to Dover. *(John May)*

1987

On 17th September the new *Pride of Dover* went off service for a mini-refit at which time the ship deputised for her on the Calais station. With the formation of P&O European Ferries in October, the ship was renamed *Pride of Walmer*.

1991

The ship operated the final Dover - Zeebrugge passenger sailing on 31st December at 18.30 with the 00.30 return on 1st January 1992. (note: P&O Stena Line reinstated passenger sailings, on a seasonal-only basis, in 2001-02 before they closed the route).

Above: Dressed overall, the **Pride of Walmer** is pictured off the Belgian coast en-route to Dover. *(Mike Louagie)*

Left: The **Pride of Walmer** at berth 5 in Dover. *(Mike Louagie)*

1992

As from 5th January the ship was switched to Dover - Calais until 26th March when she transferred to the Dover - Boulogne service on which she completed her Dover-based operations. She finally left Dover for a Falmouth refit on 5th June when the *Pride of Hythe* replaced her from the Calais route. Renamed *Pride of Rathlin*, the ship took up the 23.00 Larne - Cairnryan service (replacing the *Ionic Ferry*, ex *Dragon*) on 11th June.

The *Pride of Walmer* leaves Dover for Zeebrugge. *(Miles Cowsill)*

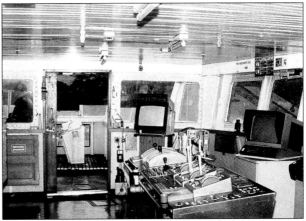

The *Pride of Rathlin's* bridge photographed when the ship was alongside at Cairnryan. *(John Hendy)*

1994

On 27th January the ship sustained grounding damage at Larne as a result of which she lost a rudder and fouled a propeller. During a subsequent dry dock survey at Belfast, tailshaft damage was discovered.

1996

Early in the year work was carried out to improve seating in the Club Class using reclining seating from the Felixstowe-based *Pride of Suffolk* and *Pride of Flanders*. The tea bar was also replaced using seating from the same ships which had reverted to ro-ro mode.

1998

Returned to service on 1st March after refit at Harland & Wolff and re-registered in Hamilton (Bermuda).

2000

With the new ro-pax *European Causeway* in service, the *Pride of Rathlin* completed service on 11th September under the command of Captain Morris Austin. She operated the 21.30 from Larne after which, with her passenger certificate expiring at midnight, she returned 'light ship' to destore before sailing to Harland & Wolff at Belfast to lay-up. Offered for sale for $1 million the vessel was sold for less than that figure to Indonesian owners

The **Pride of Rathlin's** port bridge wing. *(John Hendy)*

Above: This view shows the club class lounge on the upper deck aft of the funnel on the **Pride of Rathlin**. *(John Hendy)*

Below: The **Pride of Rathlin** arrives at Larne during her penultimate day in service with P&O in September 2000. *(John Hendy)*

Sungi Budi of Jakarta on 3rd November and returned to anchor off Larne, with all P&O markings painted out, on 10th November. Renamed *BSP III*, she entered the port for the final time three days later to load fuel tankers for her voyage eastwards. The ship left on the evening of 13th November.

2001

In service between the islands of Java and Sumatra but again offered for sale in 2002 for an optimistic $2.5 million.

Free Enterprise VIII
Pride of
Canterbury

The ship was not an exact repeat of the previous four ships being some 6 metres longer (this representing one car space) and being constructed in IHC's Verolme Shipyard at Alblasserdam rather than at Schiedam. She was also the only one of the 'Townsend Eight' not to appear with the pale green hull which failed to show up the white painted company name along it. It was believed by some that the ship was too long for Calais and consequently she primarily remained on the Zeebrugge link until the new berths were built in the French port. In 1987 she was switched to Boulogne in place of the *Free Enterprise IV*. As the last of the 'Townsend Eight' her career was fairly uneventful and she was the only ship of the series to remain operating from her port of registry throughout her entire period of UK service.

1974
Launched at Alblasserdam on 6th April by Mrs. Brenda Wickenden, wife of Group Managing Director Keith Wickenden. Maiden voyage (Captain Jack Dawson) from Dover to Zeebrugge on 18th July (due the previous day) running the 11.35 and 23.35

The final ship in the series was the *Free Enterprise VIII.* She was launched on 6th April 1974 and completed her maiden voyage to Zeebrugge on 18th July. *(John Hendy's collection)*

The *Free Enterprise VIII* is seen shortly after entering service on the Dover-Zeebrugge route. *(FotoFlite)*

The *Free Enterprise VIII* inward bound at Zeebrugge in Townsend Thoresen livery. *(Mike Louagie)*

cycle. With the Calais and Zeebrugge services only requiring seven ships with which to run them, her appearance at Dover saw the FE III switched to the North Channel.

1983

Accommodation uprated to come in line with the new 'Spirit' class.

1987

The ship deputised on the Boulogne route for the FE IV and FE V during their New Year refits. At this time the Calais ship *Herald of Free Enterprise* was switched to run her Zeebrugge roster. With the formation of P&O European Ferries in October the ship was renamed *Pride of Canterbury*. She arrived back from overhaul on 28th October and was the first unit to appear in the full P&OEF livery. Her Boat Deck passenger cabins were removed and converted to a lounge in readiness for her transfer to the Boulogne route. Following the arrival of the *Pride of Calais* and the

subsequent withdrawal of the FE IV on the morning of 4th December, the ship was transferred to the Boulogne route for the remainder of her career.

1988

During January the ship damaged her stern at Boulogne while berthing at No. 13 during strong winds. On her way to Vlissingen for repairs she lost part of her damaged rudder as a result of which she navigated stern first to dry dock at Calais. The ship remained in

The *Free Enterprise VIII* arrives at Zeebrugge sporting the P&O house flag on her funnel prior to the demise of the Townsend Thoresen name in October 1987. *(Mike Louagie)*

Calais during the long NUS strike which commenced later in the month. During April she was offered for sale. The ship finally resumed Boulogne sailings on 19th August.

1990

A new 140 seater lounge was built at her after end in the area

A late afternoon scene at Dover with the *Pride of Canterbury* outward bound for Boulogne and the *Cote d'Azur* at berth 6. *(Mike Louagie)*

Two former Dover partners together at the Island of Paros: the old Ostend ship *Express Athina* (ex *Prins Philippe*) and the *Romilda* (ex *Free Enterprise VIII*). *(Miles Cowsill)*

previously occupied by cabins.

1993

With the closure of the Dover - Boulogne route 'with immediate effect' on 4th January the ship sailed to Tilbury to lay-up and was offered for sale. She closed the link with the 06.45 ex Boulogne. Purchased in April by Nisyros Shipping of Piraeus (GA Ferries) who renamed her *Romilda*. She initially operated on the company's Adriatic route but was soon switched to an Aegean service linking Piraeus - Patmos - Leros - Kalymnos - Kos and Rhodes. The vessel has since received major structural modifications, particularly at the stern.

2002

In service (Maltese flag)

Memories of the Townsend Eight

John Hendy writes:

One memory that has always remained firmly fixed in my mind dates from April 1962. On hearing that the new *Free Enterprise* was in port, I cycled down to the sea front at Dover to catch sight of her for the first time. She had only recently arrived from Schiedam and was at the shore end of the Eastern Arm, presently occupied by berth 1. The sun was right behind her and it was low water so that one was only able to determine the shape of her superstructure against the glare of the light. Even then it was noticeable that her profile was unlike that of any other vessel then operating from Dover. With short twin funnels, she was a squat little ship and was about as different from the old *Halladale* as any vessel could be.

Later that season I viewed the *Free Enterprise* from the cliff top above the Eastern Car Ferry Terminal. She was leaving as the other vessel of 1962 was arriving from Ostend. This was the Belgian Marine car ferry *Koningin Fabiola* which presented a tremendous sight with her traditional sweeping, long, lean looks. What a contrast she presented as she passed the Townsend ship which was so much shorter and beamier.

They had been built for different eras and certainly for quite different trades.

Miles Cowsill writes:

The vessels of British Rail, SNCF and Belgian Marine were of great interest to me during my school years, however my greatest fascination was always for the green-hulled vessels with their distinctive red and black funnels. The *Free Enterprise I* was a favourite with her very modern looks and accommodation. This was possibly one of the reasons for Townsend's success and impact on the ferry industry during the sixties and seventies.

On one day trip to Calais on the FEI, I can recall having to return with BR for the first time on the *Lord Warden* and thinking to myself how old fashioned she was compared to the Townsend fleet.

Captain Bob Blowers writes:

I joined Townsend Car Ferries as 2nd Officer (Deck) for the summer season of 1964 sailing with Captain Dawson's watch. Having just come from nine years of relatively relaxing 'deep-sea' sailing with Andrew Weir's Bank Line, the change could not have been more dramatic - with continuous collision-avoidance assessment and manoeuvres during the 90 minute crossing, four dockings each period of duty and the highly intensive loading and discharging in port with as little as a 45 minute turn-round on occasion.

With a one ship service to Calais, with sailings at only six hour intervals, there was continuous pressure to maximise the car capacity of the ship with the result that no space could afford to be lost so that cars often had to be lifted by the crew into position to squeeze the last ones in.

You came to know many of the coach drivers, couriers and regular travellers - a feature that regrettably became increasingly rare as the fleet expanded. Similarly relations with the various shore personnel on both sides of the channel were generally very pleasant and convivial.

After a winter away on the southern North Sea with B.R. at Harwich (sailing on the *Colchester, Isle of Ely, Norfolk Ferry* and *Arnhem*) I served the following season (1965) as Chief Officer on the now renamed FE I with Captain Dawson. This year saw the introduction of the FE II which to us at this time looked huge and luxurious in comparison to her smaller sister. In addition to all my other duties, I was very busy this year learning to 'drive' the ship in and out of port. I found this ship-handling was often difficult and challenging but extremely satisfying when you got it exactly right.

The FE I was a wonderful ship in which to learn the necessary skills as she had the very favourable twin-screw and twin-rudder arrangement together with controllable-pitch propellers which made her a real pleasure to handle. The main problem at this time was the shallowness of Calais Harbour and Dover's Camber berths at low water which made it difficult to stop on occasion.

In those days with relatively shallow draught vessels, it was possible to take a short cut and pass over the sand bank off Calais when the tide was high enough. The French Captains on the SNCF vessel *Compiegne* were particularly knowledgeable on this subject and would cross the bank when we would feel we had to go round. The rule-of-thumb for us was whether the concrete was visible on the end of the pier. If you could see it you went round rather than over.

Having been 'kept-on' for the winter this time, I found that my duties alternated between sailing as Second Officer on the Calais off-turn i.e. single sailing from Calais to Dover and return - thus spending the night on board in Calais - and acting as Officer-in-charge of the FE II laid-up in the very exposed Prins Filip Dock in Zeebrugge.

I remember being very grateful that Captain Oliver Elsom, who I relieved, had in addition to putting out 'hurricane' moorings also had the wisdom to hang-off an anchor and put out a bite of anchor cable around one the bollards on the quay. With the ship light and riding high in the water and the water in the dock almost up to ground level, there were many nights of severe gales when this extreme measure proved to be vital to the ship's security. Incidentally, during this time I assisted our Superintendent, Captain Hendrickse, to survey a large pontoon which later became our means of discharging vehicles in the lock upon the inauguration of the Dover - Zeebrugge service.

Rozelle Raynes writes:

I grew to realise that our ship's company was like a big family with Jack Dawson as its father. On an ordinary day he put total trust in his officers and quartermasters, and it was often hard to trace his whereabouts as he had so many crew members and passengers to visit. But the first time we ran into a thick fog, I well remember Tubby Groves, the quartermaster whose face resembled a full moon, pausing at the Purser's Office on his way down from the bridge.

"You must be having a difficult watch up there, aren't you Tubby?" Muriel Chambers (the Head Purser) remarked peering through the porthole at the grey blanket of mist beyond.

"It don't matter how thick it gets with the Old Man on the bridge," he replied feelingly, "he's a bloody marvel in weather like this!"

It grew thicker every hour and during the last voyage back from Calais you could hardly see one end of the ship from the other. Jack Dawson never left the bridge that day, there was no time for Captain's rounds nor pleasant little chats with passengers. This was the real thing, the time when he came into his own; and every single person aboard that ship was depending on his skill and judgement to bring them safely home.

Captain Bob Blowers writes:

The year 1965 saw the introduction of the FE III and my promotion to Chief Officer of the FE I and Acting Master during the summer season (with Capt. Elsom as Senior Master). If we thought the FE II was huge, the FE III seemed gigantic, much better looking with her well-balanced funnel and even more luxurious inside. With the FE III entering service, one of her Masters was taken sick and I had to step in at very short notice to cover. My ship handling experience being solely confined to the FE I, I was somewhat apprehensive of such a big leap into the unknown and begged the Master I was relieving for information on the ship's handling characteristics. He said that being so much heavier, the ship carried her way frighteningly at low water and that the handles had to be on zero at least 400 yards from the berth in order to stop - even with her enormous power. It was a huge challenge but I was glad to return to the FE I and gain experience out of the spotlight.

In 1967 I became Chief Officer/Relief Master of the FE II sailing with Captain Bruce who was a very swashbuckling figure. It was he who introduced me to the alternative route to Zeebrugge via the Dunkirk and Ostend coastal route through the sand banks. This was only possible at high water and a favourable tide but it could be useful in heavy weather to get into and stay

A bird's eye view of *Free Enterprise I*. This view captures her excellent deck layout. *(FotoFlite)*

in calm water for a longer period.

Although the FE III was designed to carry freight in the side alleyways it was an extremely tight turn to get the so called 'juggernauts' in. This was assisted by a large baulk of timber at the mouth of the alleyway which was greased up with soft soap to slide the wheels into the correct position. She also had a height restriction of 13 foot 2 inches (in old money) which was very tight with tall or unladen vehicles.

During Sunday rounds one early morning, on a whim I opened up a life-jacket locker and a Steward pitched out from where he was snatching forty winks standing up. I don't know who was most surprised. On another occasion the Chief Steward reported to Captain Bruce that an assistant steward had 'jumped-ship' in Calais.

Later it turned out that the steward, who was a student working during the holiday season, had been talking to an attractive young lady during the voyage and that she had confided that she was going to drive down to the Riviera in her little sports car and spend a fortnight in her parents' empty villa - and wouldn't he like to come too? Not having his passport with him he had walked up the ramp in Calais in his steward's jacket, through the control points and into the waiting car the other side and away. Captain Bruce refused to take any disciplinary action against the steward saying that the young man would have been leaving shortly and that he himself would have done the same at his age anyway.

In 1968/69 I was Chief Officer/Acting Master of the FE III, again with Captain Elsom and sailing mainly as Master on the Zeebrugge route. The ship with her 'father & son' engines was quite fast with a good 21 knots and could achieve under four hour passages, pierhead to molehead, in favourable conditions.

One nasty experience was as a result of waiting outside Zeebrugge for a very delayed entry signal with a NW gale setting us down towards the beach. We tried to turn first to port and then to starboard with no result and finally had to unlock the

The *Free Enterprise III* is launched at Schiedam on 14th May 1966. *(John Hendy's collection)*

bow-rudder and reverse into safer waters.

John Hendy writes:
As a sixth former at Dover Boys' Grammar School, I

remember writing to Townsend to ask if I could be included on the guest list for the *Free Enterprise II's* press voyage in May 1965. Much to my surprise my request was accepted but this was the easy bit - I then had to ask my Headmaster for the day off. To his great credit he granted permission, perhaps recognising a degree of enthusiasm which he hoped might eventually spread to other, more academic, areas.

It was a wonderful early summer's day with a deep blue sky and the Dover Strait was like a mill pond. The ramparts of Cap Blanc Nez were clearly visible before we left the port and I shall always remember being asked by the motoring correspondent of one of the daily newspapers (who had obviously consumed a few too many drams before departure time) if the cliffs we could see ahead were the those of the Isle of Wight.

Rozelle Raynes writes:

One afternoon a full north-westerly gale was blowing and Captain Dawson experienced some difficulty in bringing the *Free Enterprise* into her berth at Calais owing to the surge in the outer harbour. He was a genius at docking in difficult conditions but that day he brought the ship to a halt a few yards farther away than usual on account of the wind and the swell. The seaman on the poop deck had a hard time throwing the heaving-line far enough to reach the shore and one of the Calais mooring-party men leaned forward to catch it. He trod on something slippery and lost his balance, falling head first into the harbour. A moment later he had disappeared from sight beneath the heaving oily waves, with the ship's propellers thrashing around a short distance away from his body.

A cry of despair went up from the rest of the mooring-party and someone shouted that he could not swim. Obviously there

was no time to lose and one of our seamen, Reg Stedman, did not pause for one second. He dived into the water knowing full well that he might be crushed by the enormous steel bulk of the ship's hull as it lunged against the quayside in the swell. A quartermaster, Ben Ashton, soon appeared on the scene and between them they grabbed the Frenchman, who had lost consciousness by then, and dragged him to a rope ladder that had been lowered over the starboard quarter; and two minutes later they were all hoisted to safety aboard our ship.

The Calais dock-workers organised a collection to buy some special gifts for Ben and Reg and they were presented with medals for bravery by the local Chamber of Commerce.

John Hendy writes:

The opening of the Zeebrugge route in March 1966 provided a wonderful day excursion from Dover. As a student I would regularly pay my 45s. (£2.25) and join the *Free Enterprise III* for her midday departure. During the winter period very few passengers travelled and it was almost like sailing in a private yacht. The canal entrance at Zeebrugge was reached at 16.00 where one experienced the delight of watching the town's rabbit population happily munching the rich Belgian grass either side of the berth. A quick walk around the port (which in those days was almost totally undeveloped) was followed by an 18.30 departure, an excellent meal and an arrival back in Dover at 22.30.

The Townsend ships possessed rather spartan interiors and an open plan design. If too many passengers were travelling then life on board could become rather rowdy. On one occasion coming back from Zeebrugge, the Deal Girl Pipers (not an internationally known group it must be admitted) happened to be travelling and some bright spark (was it the Purser?) suggested that they might like to 'entertain' the other passengers.

That evening the crossing seemed rather longer than usual.

Captain Bob Blowers writes:

In late 1969, with the FE IV newly in service and the FE V about to be launched, I was appointed Senior Master of the FE II. In February 1970, following the merger with Thoresen Car Ferries, I had to take the ship down to Southampton and Cherbourg for berthing trials as the linkspan arrangements were different to Dover.

Then in March, to the best of my knowledge, we became the first Townsend ship to sail to Boulogne as a result of berth congestion in Calais over the Easter weekend. This was very

Captain Dawson and the crew of the **Free Enterprise**. *(Commodore J.E. Dawson's collection)*

kindly facilitated by B.R. Sealink in acting as our agents in Boulogne and supplying us with one of their Masters (Captain Mike Bodiam) to liaise and advise on Pilotage matters.

Then in June 1970 we commenced the Southampton-Cherbourg service for Thoresen with a blaze of publicity. Unfortunately, this was followed just over a month later by a real blaze when there was a crankcase explosion on the port main engine which injured three of the engine room staff. The vessel was left immobilised twenty-one miles off Cherbourg and so assistance was required. Helicopters were unavailable but a French minesweeper gallantly tried to come alongside to take off the injured - which in the event proved impossible owing to a heavy sea running.

Eventually a large French navy tug reached us and towed us in to Cherbourg, the passengers and vehicles eventually disembarking some twelve hours after the incident. After emergency repairs, the vessel left for Rotterdam to carry out full repairs. Subsequently all such engines were fitted with detection equipment to lessen the chance of further crankcase explosions.

Because our berth in Cherbourg was on the lee side of a very exposed pier and the FE II with her twin screw/single rudder set-up had very little 'screwing' ability, it was necessary to run a gantline along the ship's side from aft and to throw an attached heaving line from the fo'csle as we passed the end of the jetty. Consequently we always managed to cope there and in Southampton we experimented with reversing the port main engine on engine-room control to assist our required manoeuvre - although this proved to be problematical and was abandoned.

All this summer I was studying hard to take the Southampton

The *Free Enterprise VIII* makes an impressive view outward bound from Dover. *(FotoFlite/ by courtesy of Captain Bob Blowers)*

Pilotage examination and most of the pilots that we carried at this time were generously helpful with all the little wrinkles and lore that are so necessary for a knowledge of such a large and complex area. When I sat the examination, I had been advised that the Senior Pilot 'liked' to catch a candidate out and effortlessly I was able to oblige him on a couple of luckily fairly minor details.

Regrettably obtaining the license meant that I became involved in politics in that in January 1971, I was required to sign on the Norwegian flag *Viking 1* as 1st Officer and carry out the pilotage duties for a period of 2 weeks. Apart from the embarrassment of doing the pilots out of a job, I thoroughly enjoyed my time on the ship and was amazed how efficiently she was run on what was admittedly a less intensive service than I was used to.

Because of her lack of freight capacity FE II (max. height: 11' 2") was again laid up for the winter - this time in Bruges. To do so, it was necessary to transit the Zeebrugge - Bruges canal, a journey not for the faint hearted with a light-ship, a fresh beam wind and a narrow, rickety swing-bridge to pass through. Once there though she was very secure.

I was employed during the winter 1970/71 as leave Relief Master on the new and seemingly very splendid FE V with Captain Dawson again - always a stimulating experience.

1971 was a repeat, though happily uneventful, season with the FE II at Southampton - this time with myself piloting the ship during my week on duty. Every once in a while we used to leave Cherbourg immediately after the *Queen Elizabeth 2*. Once in the large outer harbour, we used to call 'QE 2 this is FE II please may we pass?' On receiving the affirmative we would enjoy whistling past her at our full 18.5 knots and proceed on our way to Southampton via the Needles. The QE 2 had to go the longer route via the Nab Tower but she was always passing the Bramble Bank some ten miles ahead of us coming up from the opposite direction.

We were always very aware of the problems of wash effect if the vessel went too fast in certain locations and this was one of the factors in favour of the later move to Portsmouth. I remember on one occasion with a pilot on board when we were following the *Nieuw Amsterdam* (36,000 tons) out to the west and passing Cowes I.O.W. The pilot was chortling as waves (wash from the liner) could be clearly seen coming over the sea wall at Cowes until I pointed out that anyone looking out would only see the FE II as the other ship was by then out of sight.

Late that year the FE II in her lay-berth in Bruges was painted up in the new Townsend livery of darker green hull so that she was looking her best when she was required for a very unusual charter arrangement. Apparently the usual 'Motor Racing Show' had been cancelled and the charterers were looking for an alternative and exciting venue. The ship was required to load up in Dover with racing cars and a great deal of other promotional material and proceed to the Pool of London and moor up alongside the veteran cruiser HMS *Belfast* on New Year's Eve This was all extremely interesting and a great experience (later repeated in 1981 with the *Pride of Free Enterprise*) although this initial time we were designated the 'Motor Racing Showboat' and were open daily to the public for the next nine days before proceeding back via Dover to lay-up again.

John Hendy writes:

A visit to Southampton in July 1984 found the sale-listed *Free Enterprise III* tucked away in the Empress Dock. Having been given permission to look around the ship and take photographs, Miles Cowsill and I arrived at Townsend Thoresen's offices in order to be issued with the necessary paperwork. The ship manager informed us that we were very fortunate as the ferry was in the process of being sold and would soon be leaving. The obvious questions were, to whom and to where and these were duly asked. We were promptly informed that such information was *strictly* between the buyer and seller and was certainly not for public consumption as it could be prejudicial to the sale. This point was expanded and amplified to such an extent that by the time that we finally left the office and made our way across to the ship, one was certainly left with the impression that it had been foolish to have wasted time by asking such questions in the first place.

Eventually we climbed on board the *Free Enterprise III* to be met by the watchman who greeted us with the words, "You're only just in time - she's been sold to Malta."

Captain Vic Ridges writes:

I arrived in Dover in June 1976 for an interview with Townsend Car Ferries regarding employment. The offices were at that time in a converted house in Camden Crescent near the sea front. I had held a Masters' Certificate for the previous seven years and like many of my contemporaries at the time I was newly married, deep sea work was becoming less attractive and I wanted employment that would give me some home life. It all sounded wonderful - 7 x 12 hour day duties and 7 x 12 hour night duties over a 28 day period.

the Townsend eight

The *Free Enterprise II* laid up in the inner dock at Calais in 1980. *(Captain Vic Ridges)*

The next day I found myself reporting to the *Free Enterprise II* to do my first 'makee learn' (ferry language) and after a couple of days I was on my own as Second Officer. Previously I had been on passenger ships on 'Round the World' voyages but the FE II was like nothing that I had ever seen or sailed on before.

Firstly she was, by anyone's standards, small. Neither was she a pretty ship; the rounded bow saw to that and to add insult to injury there was a bridge at each end! There were other peculiar features such as two sets of navigation lights - one set for each direction. By day black balls hoisted at the main mast indicated that the vessel was navigating stern first (see the splendid photo inside the back cover of JH's book 'Ferry Port Dover').

She was extremely well looked-after and smart - helped by the fact that she only worked from April to September - and had a very enthusiastic and caring team led by Captain Clive Wood

(one of the few officers from that era who are still working). Her smartness and cleanliness was in no small part due to the fact that she was a pure car ferry - the only one in the fleet. She did not, nor could not, carry those dirty things that had so prospered the development of the company - freight! However, one type of freight vehicle that we could accommodate were the wine tankers of the French haulier 'Giraud.' These were short and, with a little help from soapy water to get the trailer wheels to slide around the tight manoeuvre, were just able to negotiate the alleyways on either side of the ship.

When I joined her, the FE II was already ten years old. I don't know at what stage the aft bridge had ceased to be used and became redundant but by 1976 it was used as a store for spare LSA and FFA equipment and general junk. Everything was of course disconnected but someone had left the door unlocked and some children got in. Unbelievably the 'emergency stop' buttons for the main engines were still connected and yes, you've guessed it, they were pushed and the ship stopped. Passengers were a rule unto themselves in those days, they seemed to get everywhere but no one seemed to mind. The FE II was something akin to a holiday ferry as she only carried tourist traffic.

Because of her dimensions, loading the FE II was, I soon discovered, an art form in itself. Car caravans, camping vans and coaches all had to arrive on board in the correct order and woe betide if something arrived that was too big! To help prevent this we had ashore aluminium poles in the shape of an inverted 'L' which were put alongside a coach or other high vehicle before loading. Most of the coaches of today would not have fitted. Even the simple two axle coaches of 25 years ago were a tight fit and it was necessary to check that the vents on top were closed. The likely consequence of leaving a vent open was for it to strike a

An unusual view of the *Free Enterprise III* leaving Dover Western Docks for Boulogne while on charter to Sealink in July 1981. Notice the Sealink houseflag on her main mast. To be in line with other units of the railway fleet, the Sealink Masters nick-named her 'Earl Wickenden.' *(Andrew Jones)*

The *Free Enterprise VII* laid up in the Granville Dock at Dover in December 1984. *(Andrew Jones)*

sprinkler head and soak everyone in the coach. And it happened - ask retired Master John Farringdon.

From the above it is obvious that the FE II was far short of being a success and to me it was surprising that the next TTF ferry to be built (the FE III) was exactly on the same lines although larger and with sufficient headroom to carry some freight.

One Saturday morning during my first few weeks at Dover I arrived with Chief Officer Chris Double to find that we were boarding not our usual steed but the FE I which had been laid-up in the West Dock at Calais all summer. During the previous night the FE II had been caught by the wind while berthing at Calais number 4 and had damaged her bow visor which was in the process of being raised. Captain Dave Simpson was the unfortunate Master in command at the time. (note: the FE II had two propellers with VP controlled from the bridge. However with only one single stern rudder, this made manoeuvring extremely difficult in bad weather.)

For those of us unfamiliar with her at the time, stepping on board the FE I was another experience. Our uniforms were on board the FE II on the other side of the Channel in Roglianos shipyard in Carnot Dock, Calais. But it was Saturday morning in high summer and all sailings were fully booked and so the FE I just *had* to sail with a mainly unfamiliar crew, mostly, including me, dressed in 'civvies'! On our arrival in Calais a bus was laid on to take us to the stricken FE II being repaired at the shipyard. At least we now had our uniforms.

Loading the FE I was a whole new ball game! With no bow door, getting the tractor trailers down the extremely narrow linkspans in reverse was another art form - some freight drivers would rather wait for the next ship than attempt it! However, a few days later the FE II resumed service and the FE I was returned to the West Dock at Calais to resume her lay-up. Of course the above events of 25 years ago would not be tolerated today!

In this my first brief encounter with the FE I, one aspect of the operation surprised me. One arrival at Calais - whatever the weather conditions - the ship swung outside in 'the roads' before entering the port stern first. For the poor old Second Mate aft, you were very likely to get soaked from the seas breaking over the stern. Ducking into the galley to keep dry was a dodge I soon learned! Just why the Masters did this manoeuvre is still a mystery to me as there was plenty of room to enter normally (bow first) and swing off the Quai Paul Devot. JH suggests that this was a carry-over from the way that the railway steam ships entered port.

At the end of the 1976 season, in late September the FE II was 'put to bed' for the winter and laid-up at Tilbury. The FE IV arrived from the Irish Sea and the FE II's crew transferred to her. The FE I also ended up laid-up alongside the FE II at Tilbury. They were both 'dead ships' and were looked after during the day by one deck and one engineer officer. When it was my turn to do a stint at Tilbury it was a lonely job and a low point of my career.

And so ended my first months in the ferry trade. With the FE IV, at last there was a radical design change and the naval architects, after three false starts, were getting it right.

At Easter 1977 it all started again. The FE II came out of her winter sleep to earn her living for the summer and as the FE IV

An unusual view of the ***Pride of Walmer*** deputising at Boulogne following the closure of the Zeebrugge passenger service at the end of 1991. *(Nicholas Meads)*

had returned to the Irish Sea, the FE I also became operational although at the beginning and end of the high season. She ran only during the day and laid-up at night with the same crew ie they did a 24 hour duty. The colloquial name for it was the 'off turn'. She wasn't designed for the crew to live even one night aboard and so I, along with others, was quite happy when that system of operation was over!

I remained with the FE I/ FE II circuit until the FE I made her final crossing on Christmas Eve 1979 and she was sold. Her departure was somewhat overshadowed by the arrival of the *Spirit of Free Enterprise*. By that time I was Chief Officer and had transferred to the FE III which gained the new title of 'oldest ship in the fleet.' It was the FE II all over again but bigger! By the way we had the same problem with sprinklers being hit by high vehicles. It was such a common incident that we even had a 'Golden Sprinkler Award' (a golden sprinkler mounted on a piece of polished wood) given monthly to the Officer who most caused this occurrence. Chief Officer Reg Hallet held it almost continuously!

I served on all the 'Free Enterprise' ships and from August to December 1989 I was on what was to be my last FE - the FE VIII which was by then the *Pride of Canterbury*. I was serving as Senior Chief Officer with Senior Master Captain Graham Thorne to get my 'second pass' as Master. I left with my 'pass' in December 1989 (to return to my ship the *Pride of Dover*) and never set foot on an FE again.

Miles Cowsill writes:

During the early seventies, I was to spend a considerable amount of time travelling on the Zeebrugge service, sailing very regularly on the *Free Enterprise IV* and *Free Enterprise V*, over a three-year period of regular visits to Brussels. Each four hour crossing had something different to offer including many interesting visits to the bridge. On one of these trips there were only five passengers on the 08.30 sailing to Zeebrugge and everyone was invited to breakfast at one table in the Dining Room for a a 'full house' on the company- typically Townsend and something which I sure none of us will be ever be able to experience again!

Captain Bob Blowers writes:

With the introduction of the FE VII in 1973, I took over as Senior Master of the FE V, a vessel with excellent ship-handling characteristics and one I was already very familiar with. The only

Pictured with the ***Free Enterprise V*** immediately after her launch are (l. to r.) Captains David Bruce, Gilbert Saunders, Jack Dawson and Bob Blowers. *(Captain Bob Blowers collection)*

slight problem with the ship was that, in common with her post FE I predecessors, she was fitted with 'Flume' type tank stabilisers, which we were advised were designed by students from Rotterdam University. It must have been 'rag-week' when they did it because in bad weather with a load of heavy lorries, she had to be nursed along very carefully to avoid any damage. For instance going to Calais in a SW gale necessitated steering east for as long as possible until the rolling got too heavy - then steer south at slow speed with the wind four points on the starboard bow - making good about SE until in the lee of Cap Griz Nez - then hard round and steer straight for Calais at full speed.

On another occasion there was a terrible NNE gale, storm force 10 - 12 and on getting clear of Zeebrugge, we were unable to steer our usual westerly course (we tried twice and the ship nearly turned over) and so had to continue at dead slow speed to the north until finally we came north of the North Hinder light vessel (on the approaches to Rotterdam) and were able to put the wind astern and turn onto our required south westerly course. The wind then veered to NW and almost immediately superimposed a huge north westerly swell on top of the still very evident NNE'ly swell. We corkscrewed our way home at full speed and the only damage to the cargo was where some metal pieces had come through the side of one particular lorry.

Passengers couldn't have enjoyed the voyage and certainly none of the crew did. Later I found out that the town of Deal had been flooded by the sea breaking through the sea walls in this same gale.

Showing off her new livery, the **Free Enterprise V** laid up on the Eastern Arm at Dover on Boxing Day 1975. *(John May)*

I spent the next five years on the FE V on a routine of nine months on the Zeebrugge route followed by three on the Calais run. This was fairly incident free until in March 1977 we received an emergency call from a small coaster, *Tower Venture* on fire to the north of the shipping lanes off Ostend. We arrived at the ship and, together with the *European Trader*, sent over trained firefighters and fighting equipment in the ship's lifeboat. It became apparent that the fire could not be put out with the limited equipment available and so I decided that the weather conditions would just allow us to close the small vessel and pass fire hoses across to their stern so that we could turn on our pumps.

On the *Tower Venture*, and under the control of our Chief Officer Pat MacWilliam, two of our crewmen Alex Black and Duncan Denny entered the engine room wearing breathing apparatus and eventually put the fire out with the hoses. This took some time and it was quite difficult keeping the ship in position to deploy the hoses. Once again I'm afraid that the few passengers we were carrying on this night sailing got back to Dover somewhat later than scheduled.

Entering Calais early one morning, there was an emergency in the engine room and we lost all the three main engines and bow thruster. Fortunately we still had the use of the rudder and so could steer, however it was low water and the basin was full of ships and so an attempt to bring the ship to a premature halt with both anchors could cause us to collide with one or other of the vessels. So both anchors were dropped but only one shackle veered out. By this means we hoped to slow the ship sufficiently to land gently in our berth and get our moorings out. It nearly

The **Romilda** (ex **Free Enterprise VIII**) seen in the Aegean in September 2001 en-route from Santorini to the Island of Naxos. *(Miles Cowsill)*

worked! We hit the very forgiving spring-loaded pads with our 'spade' belting forward with a bit of a thump and damage to the ship and shore installation was negligible. Passengers and crew had all been thoroughly alerted by the public address system to sit down and hold tight and so no one was caught unawares.

In 1978, on the transfer of the *Viking Valiant* to the Dover service, I once again took over a ship from Captain Dawson - this time the *Free Enterprise VIII*. Initially I was not all that keen to move to what I thought would be a very similar ship but I was to

find out that the newer Werkspoor-engined ship was a big improvement on the FE V. She was a little longer, having larger and improved vehicle drivers' accommodation, she was faster and most importantly had really excellent and reliable fin-stabilisers which enabled the vessel to steer almost any desired course in bad weather.

The exception was an extremely severe SW'ly gale, forecasted well in advance but late to arrive. I remember being in Zeebrugge with not a drop of wind and a shore manager asking why Captain

Saunders had just ordered a tug for his arrival in the FE III. By the time we had reached the Mole it was blowing force 6 and by the Zand Entrance Buoy, force 8. The FE III never did get to Zeebrugge that night and had to heave-to way north of Ostend in very heavy sea conditions. With her excellent fin stabilisers I was confident that the FE VIII could manage but near where the FE III was hove-to we ran clear of coast and sandbanks and into the full severity of the sea and swell.

The FE VII was about to follow us out of Zeebrugge at about that time and knowing that their stabilisers were out of action, I alerted the Master to the true severity of the weather, which helped him to decide to delay his sailing.

There was no way we could follow the strict letter of the routeing requirements and proceed from there in a WNW'ly direction so we, in company with the FE V and later the FE III slowly headed in a SW'ly direction down between the sandbanks and the NE shipping lane. Needless to say in such weather other shipping was minimal.

One of the strange coincidences of that night was that every ship bar one had the Senior Master on duty. The one exception being Captain Dawson who was tucked up in bed at home rather than on the *Viking Valiant* - but then he has always had a special guiding star.

I handed over the FE VIII at the end of 1979 in preparation for going out to Bremerhaven to standby the newbuilding *Pride of Free Enterprise*.

Captain Alan Ewart-James writes:
The *Free Enterprise VIII* proved to be a very versatile ship.

Being the last and longest of the 'FE' breed she was considered too big to run into Calais and was thus put on the Zeebrugge passenger run for a number of years.

With the development of Calais to take larger ships she was later switched to that route but with the Townsend Thoresen takeover of P&O Normandy Ferries, she was eventually switched to the Boulogne route in place of the smaller *nf Tiger* and *nf Panther* which were later disposed of.

The ship operated this route for a number of years, sometimes going stern up to No.16 berth in Boulogne but normally running bow up to No. 13 berth. Boulogne can at times be a very awkward port to get into as it lies on the lee shore of the prevailing SW winds and during stormy weather the outer breakwater can be awash with waves breaking over the lighthouse when a horrendous swell builds up right at the entrance. However once inside the inner port, the wind strength drops dramatically thanks to the shelter provided by the nearby buildings. Northerly winds however pose a problem as they come straight down the coast from Cap Gris Nez and are an off berth wind when in No. 13. However a slight change of wind to the easterly quadrant again dramatically effects the strength of the wind and can afford a lot of shelter. Unlike Calais or Dover, it was not possible to obtain an accurate wind speed and direction from Port Control and often there were no other ferries in the port to call up and enquire of the condition inside.

Thus it was on such a day in January 1988 with a brisk northerly wind blowing that I entered the port to berth in No. 13. On reaching the outer harbour I assessed that it would be possible to berth but to be on the safe side I ordered a tug to assist if necessary.

As we ran down the passage between the inner piers the wind

increased in strength and I was glad to have the tug available. I managed to manoeuvre the bow onto the pads but was not able to get the stern within about ten feet of the jetty and against the strong wind, the stern crew were unable to throw the heaving lines ashore. The tug moved alongside the stern quarter and attempted to push the ship up wind but to no avail, as the wind was increasing in strength all the time.

The second harbour tug was called for but her crew were not on standby and she was not able to assist immediately. The stern of the ship gradually drifted down wind and with a small tanker on the oil berths on the lee side of the basin, there was not enough room to abort and attempt to leave either bow or stern first. With the gallant tug still attempting to push the quarter, the stern continued drifting until such time that the *Pride of Canterbury* lay at right angles across the entrance of the Bassin Napoleon with her stern over the slipway used to haul fishing boats out of the water.

Contact with the stone work meant that the shell plating was stove in about two feet above the water line but below the belting at the shoulder of the accommodation. When the second harbour tug eventually arrived it was possible to recover from this position and berth the ship at No. 13. However, due to the damage it was decided to return in ballast for repairs at Dover by the local engineering company. Unfortunately the position of the damage was such that they declined the work and so the ship was sent instead to Vlissingen under the command of the Senior Master, Captain Graham Thorne.

Off the Sandiette Bank, en route to the Dutch port a good part of the damaged main rudder fell off and so we were diverted to Calais navigating astern all the way and using the bow rudder to steer her by. The ship eventually berthed at the Bassin Carnot

The **Free Enterprise IV** outward bound from Larne to Cairnryan. *(Ken Kane)*

and shortly afterwards the 1988 NUS strike broke out and there she remained until the strike ended.

With the ship's arrival in Calais, the crew were immediately sent to Chatham to reactivate the sale-listed *Free Enterprise IV*. When the strike broke out shortly afterwards the crews refused to load and sail the ships so they were sent to the Downs to anchor and return to Dover every twelve hours for a crew change.

One night, as I was walking across the dock at Dover to join for the night shift, I was stopped by one of the managers from our Head Office and was told that as a move in relation to this strike, some time during that night the ships were going to be dispersed to foreign ports. I was told to listen on VHF Channel 74 at 02.00 when I would receive instructions and was further told to keep this under my hat and not to give the crew any warning.

So after changing the crew we went and anchored in the Downs to await events. As 02.00 approached I was somewhat agitated as I knew what their reaction would be to the ship leaving the Dover area and as it was necessary to man the chain locker each time the anchor was weighed (the lockers being too small on the FE ships for self-stowing), I thought it prudent to be under way when the news broke.

At about 01.00 I went to the bridge and there was a strong flood tide running and a stiff SW wind. I told the Officer I was not happy with the anchorage position and so he called out the anchor party to weigh anchor. This was achieved and we stooged around until I eventually received the secret message when I was instructed to proceed to the Sunk Light Vessel to pick up a Thames pilot at 06.00 and make for Chatham from where the crew would be bussed home.

I then notified the Chief Officer, Chief Engineer and Purser of these instructions and told them to inform their crew. As I had anticipated, on hearing the news the crew were up in arms and refused to carry out orders. So with an Officer on the wheel and another manning the pilot ladder, the Thames pilot was eventually picked up. When it was obvious that I was not going to turn back to Dover as the crew had demanded, the quartermaster took over the steering but I instructed the Bridge Officer to keep a close eye on him. Off Sheerness, we had to sail very close to the sunken ammunition ship USS *Richard Montgomery* and I wanted a true course steered.

At Garrison Point the pilots changed and the Medway pilot came aboard but the pilot vessel, not being used to ferries, dropped astern from the pilot ladder and hit our stern spade.

The *Free Enterprise IV* bow in at Calais. (*John Hendy's collection*)

Fortunately no one was hurt.

After manoeuvring through the locks, we tied up in the basin at Chatham and the awaiting busses took the crew back to Dover. Apart from leaving a mess in their accommodation, not much damage had taken place apart from all the plugs having been cut off the microwave ovens. They obviously reckoned that the officers would not be able to cook without them!

So the FE IV remained in Chatham and never again sailed for P&O European Ferries.

Captain Jas. W. Martin writes:

There have been huge changes in the ferry trade during the past thirty years, not least in the size and capacity of the ships. Nothing serves better to emphasise this than to briefly compare some aspects of freight carriage in the *Free Enterprise I* with the *European Seaway* class which entered service thirty years later.

The FE I was a stern-loader and very much a first-generation vehicular ro-ro ferry, although one of the first such to be built both for the carriage of freight and tourist traffic. Semi-trailers and articulated lorries (artics) were carried in a large well on the Main Deck (and two small lorries in the entrances to her main deck alleyways!) whereas the 'Seaway' class presently carry such traffic on two uncluttered drive-through decks. Whereas the FE I could carry six artics (or up to eight if you adopted the time-consuming practice of loading each trailer part as a drop and stowing the units in the alleyways!), the 'Seaway' class accommodates at least 110 such vehicles. In short, more freight can be carried in one lane on one deck than the FE I could carry in total. The present day Mate and loading crew, whilst still under pressure on turn-round time and still needing an eye for a good stow and choice of vehicle, also have to take account of complicated segregation and the stowage requirements of the International Maritime Dangerous Goods Code.

Freight vehicles are now loaded through large bow and stern doors via double-width ramps but articulated vehicles had to be reversed aboard the FE I. Given the narrowness and length of the old-style linkspans and their steepness at dead low water, this was something that tested the competence of many drivers and which often led to heated exchanges, particularly with foreign drivers who refused to follow directions. Even more difficulty would be experienced with the occasional lorry-trailer rigs which were sometimes disconnected to allow the trailer to be backed on using the lorry's front chassis pin. Such difficulties could be overcome by using the legendary expertise of the Townsend stevedore drivers who either drove the vehicles or sometimes who replaced the tractor unit with one of our own Tugmaster units.

Since the Mate's reputation (and thus promotion prospects!) in those days depended largely on his perceived loading abilities, I belatedly acknowledge a debt to these skilled stevedore drivers and also to the Bosuns who were always on hand to offer valuable advice to inexperienced new Officers fresh from a less hectic deep-water lifestyle.

Captain Jas. W. Martin writes:

Spectators watching ferries berthing from the cliff top vantage point of Langdon Battery car park may have noticed changes in berthing methods over the years but may not have fully appreciated the reasons for this. Berthing techniques have changed to meet the requirements of larger ships and modifications to berths. This has been possible thanks to more engine power delivered via improved propellers and control systems, larger and improved rudders and not least, the provision of more powerful bow thrusters.

In the 1960's we had essentially inherited the berthing techniques from the old steam turbine packets in the Western Docks whereby they were berthed stern-first at high speed using their bow rudders and relying heavily on relatively large amounts of available ahead power to stop. In severe conditions success depended upon the skill and confidence of the Master and his Quartermaster and also on the ability of the seamen to quickly pick up off wires and shore moorings, including heavy coir springs. I have heard the story of one Southern Railway Chief

Engineer who, not trusting the judgement of a new Master, would station himself at the engine room skylight and shout the order to open the ahead steam valve in advance of receipt of the telegraph order from the bridge!

Even with the advent of narrow 'slot' car ferry berths at the Eastern Docks, these techniques continued due to the availability of bow-rudders and because, despite the introduction of controlled pitch propellers and bow thrusts, there remained inadequate control of both bow and stern in strong off-shore winds.

Arriving from the somewhat sedate Australian meat trade, I admit to being somewhat surprised at finding ships being hurled full astern at solid concrete at something approaching 15 knots! Successive 'Free Enterprise' vessels had improvements in power of bow-thrusters and the introduction of the first triple-screwed ship (FE IV) meant improved control of the stern. However, these developments were somewhat off set by much higher windage due to increased superstructure size and the previous berthing practice continued.

Thus in severe weather, for example in a SW gale at high water, ships would be taken well up the harbour almost to the Western Entrance and brought to rest with the wind right ahead. The bow rudder was then unlocked and with propellers at full astern, she would be steered for her berth allowing her to gradually drop to leeward all the time. In the latter stages of the approach, as the ship passed the end of the old West Jetty, her bow would be still in the wind as the stern gained the lee of the wind wall, at which point plenty of starboard helm was applied on the bow rudder and maximum bow thrust applied. By this time the stern would just be entering the slot berth (with only a foot or so on each side) - then and only then would ahead power be applied to stop the ship. It was not uncommon under such

circumstances for experienced Quartermasters to politely caution newly appointed Masters against taking the way off too soon!

Despite their size the 'Spirit' class (with their revolutionary bow propeller dramatically improving bow rudder steering) could be berthed stern first in moderate conditions. However, it soon became apparent that their much greater windage area warranted a change of tactic if they were to be berthed safely in strong SW gales, especially at high water. In such conditions, the technique was developed of bringing the ship head to wind, to windward of the berth and dropping down into the berth in a controlled manner. In more severe conditions, using a technique that Nelson would have recognised, the weather anchor could be dropped to aid in controlling the bow. These techniques were even more necessary as ship size increased further with the arrival of the *Pride of Dover* class and the later freight ships and turning off the berth is now the norm in most vessels.

John Hendy writes:

During April 1997, the **Ferry Publications** Scandinavian excursion included the route linking Gedser (Denmark) and Rostock (Germany) which was being operated by the *Rostock Link*, the former Townsend-Thoresen ship *European Gateway*. Imagine our surprise and delight when we arrived at Gedser to be greeted by the spare ferry *Falster Link*, the former *Free Enterprise IV* which was about to commence her final stint of service while the newer vessel went off for refit.

The ship was a time capsule and had hardly changed internally with much evidence of her original configuration and it was a heart-warming experience to clamber through her, recognising original signs, fittings and furniture. We even made our way out onto the forward passenger deck below the bridge which brought back happy memories of crossing to Zeebrugge in her Townsend days. There was a choice of two hot meals available that evening but by the time that we reached the cafeteria, there was only one - meat balls with red cabbage.

John Hendy writes:

The **Ferry Publications** excursion to the North Channel in September 2000 was primarily to sail for a final time in the *Pride of Rathlin*, the former *Free Enterprise VII*, which was about to be withdrawn. It was the first time that I had boarded her since she had left Dover in early 1992 and with the ship so close to retirement, the company had made every effort to economise during her final refit. Certain parts were very run down and the Club Class lounge behind the funnel was closed up. In spite of this the Larne crew had made every effort and showed tremendous pride in their ship which they recognised represented something special which they would never again experience.

Our party was invited to the bridge by Captain Morris Austin

as he took the ship out of Loch Ryan after which we were treated to a magnificent supper in the ro-ro drivers' dining room. It was a memorable crossing, made even more so by the generosity and thoughtfulness of the 'Rathlin's' excellent Captain and crew. A fine way indeed by which to remember the last operational member of the 'Townsend Eight' in UK waters.

Captain Morris Austin bringing the **Pride of Rathlin** astern out of the Cairnryan berth in September 2000. *(John Hendy)*

The **Pride of Rathlin** raises anchor off Larne on her penultimate day in the North Channel. *(John Hendy)*

TOWNSEND BROS. CAR FERRIES LTD. (to 1965)
TOWNSEND CAR FERRIES LTD.
TOWNSEND THORESEN CAR FERRIES LTD. (European Ferries Group)
P&O EUROPEAN FERRIES (DOVER) LTD. (from October 1987)

Name	Year	Gross tonnage	Net tonnage	Deadweight	Length	Breadth	Draft	Pass	Cars	Freight	Call Sign	Engines
FREE ENTERPRISE	1962	2607	890	457	96.47	16.39	4.1	846	120	6	GIAR	2 x Smit-MAN
FREE ENTERPRISE I	1964											
FREE ENTERPRISE II*	1965	4011	1576		108.13	18.39	4.1	998	205	0	GQMA	2 x Smit-MAN
FREE ENTERPRISE III*	1966	4657	1899	839	117.51	19.08	4.1	1114	221	14	GSNA	2 x Smit-MAN
FREE ENTERPRISE IV	1969	5049	1945	1132	117.51	19.44	4.3	1132	260	24	GZDA	3 x Smit-MAN
FREE ENTERPRISE V	1970	5044	1977	1355	117.51	19.44	4.4	1132	260	24	GNOE	3 x Smit-MAN
PRIDE OF HYTHE	1987											
FREE ENTERPRISE VI**	1972	4981	1890	1170	117.51	19.49	4.4	1132	314	24	GQAL	3 x Stork-Werkspoor
PRIDE OF SANDWICH	1987									60		
PRIDE OF AILSA***	1992											
FREE ENTERPRISE VII**	1973	4981	1892	1166	117.51	19.49	4.4	1132	314	24	GQHM	3 x Stork-Werkspoor
PRIDE OF WALMER	1987									60		
PRIDE OF RATHLIN***	1992											
FREE ENTERPRISE VIII	1974	5170	2048	1292	123.60	19.49	4.4	1101	320	27	GUEN	3 x Stork-Werkspoor
PRIDE OF CANTERBURY	1987											

* registered owners were subsidiary Stanhope SS Co, Dover. Other six ships registered under Townsend Car Ferries Ltd. Dover.

** rebuilt 1985

*** renamed when transferred to Cairnryan - Larne route